What Church Leaders Say about *Alpha*

"Out of England comes an exciting new program which is moving churches around the world from maintenance to mission. Alpha is a well-designed, implementable program that addresses the basic questions of life for the churched and unchurched alike. Through Alpha, Jesus Christ is capturing the hearts and minds of an ever-growing number of persons. The course meets the vital test of being both open and faithful—welcoming of all, while presenting the gospel message with clarity and power."

George Gallup, Jr.

Chairman, The George H. Gallup International Institute

"The Alpha Course is a most engaging way of passing on the basics of Christianity. It is a tool for evangelism and nurture that I highly recommend."

J. I. Packer

Professor of Theology, Regent College, Vancouver, Canada

"Alpha seems especially blessed in that the Lord is using it to reach all sorts of people in all sorts of spiritual conditions. Genius is the art of taking the complex and communicating it with warmth and simplicity. If you've ever wondered 'Why Jesus?' you'll hardly find a better answer than this."

Luis Palau

Evangelist

"Alpha Courses are helping to change the face of the church in the UK. Throughout the country churches are catching on to a new and fresh approach to evangelism and the nurture of new believers. From small beginnings, Alpha is now making a major impact and providing the opportunity for churches of all denominations to adopt this significant model in obeying our Lord's command to 'make disciples from every nation.' I warmly commend the whole Alpha initiative."

Clive Calver

CEO, President, World Relief Corporation

"The Alpha Course is to me another example of the ongoing need for each successive generation to express its faith in contemporary terms and on current issues. I am not surprised to hear of its immediate acceptance and use by hundreds of churches all over the world and, furthermore, of the consequent decisions for Christ that it has generated. More power to Jesus!"

John Wimber

Association of Vineyard Churches

"God has used the Alpha ministry in a significant way to reach the seeking pre-Christians of England. We, in an increasingly secularized North America, have much we can learn from the Alpha leaders about the principles which have enabled them to reach a biblically illiterate generation. I warmly commend the leaders of these conferences and the information they will present."

Leighton Ford
Leighton Ford Ministries

"Alpha has proved itself to be an effective way of exploring faith and deepening commitment to Jesus as Lord. I commend it warmly."

Nigel McCulloch
Bishop of Wakefield, Chairman of the Decade of Evangelism

"The phenomenal growth of Alpha Courses is showing the church that we do not need to be defensive about our faith, but can expect people to be interested, and then radically changed by the Gospel."

Elaine Storkey
The Institute for Contemporary Christianity

"Alpha is a soul winning, discipling, multiplying, spiritually dynamic ministry that has already touched the lives of thousands. I believe this vision will continue to expand and truly become an international blessing."

Loren Cunningham
Youth With A Mission International

"My first knowledge of the Alpha Course came from friends who witnessed its effectiveness for renewal. Now I can say first hand that Alpha is an effective tool for congregational-based evangelism and for building up the community."

Ronald H. Haines
Bishop of Washington

"The Alpha Courses are transforming churches all across Britain, showing extraordinary success in stimulating interest . . . and then real faith among the uninterested and unchurched. I am so pleased to learn the courses are being introduced to the American and Canadian churches as well. A must for anyone serious about bringing others to Christ."

John W. Howe
Bishop of Central Florida

"Alpha is the most effective means of evangelism using small groups that I know. John Wesley's class meeting rediscovered."
Rob Frost
National Evangelist, Methodist Church

"I welcome the introduction of the Alpha Conferences into the church in the United States. These conferences combine sound teaching, personal experience of Christian community, and commitment to life in the faith and will be a welcome addition to the process of renewing the church."
Peter James Lee
Bishop of Virginia

"The Alpha Course has been of enormous value to churches in strengthening fellowship and increasing effective evangelism in the local community."
David Coffey
General Secretary, The Baptist Union of Great Britian

"Nicky Gumbel loves Christ, is a student of the Word and has a passion for the things that Christ had on His heart . . . the lost and His people."
Paul Stanley
Vice President, The Navigators

"One of the most effective tools of evangelism in the body of Christ in the United Kingdom is the Alpha Course. This new and effective course has exploded, being used by hundreds of churches resulting in thousands of new believers being integrated into the local church. The enthusiasm is spreading rapidly. I wholeheartedly recommend Nicky Gumbel's excellent leadership. God has blessed the church greatly in raising up Nicky to trumpet the Alpha Course."
Mike Bickle
Metro Vineyard Fellowship, Kansas City

Nicky Gumbel

HOW TO RUN
THE ALPHA COURSE

A Handbook for Alpha Directors,
Leaders, and Helpers

Cook Ministry Resources, a division of Cook Communications Ministries
Colorado Springs, Colorado / Paris, Ontario

By the same author:
Why Jesus?
Why Christmas?
Questions of Life
Searching Issues
A Life Worth Living
Challenging Lifestyle

Cook Ministry Resources is a division of Cook Communications Ministries International (CCMI). In fulfilling its mission to encourage the acceptance of Jesus Christ as personal Savior and to contribute to the teaching and putting into practice of His two great commandments, CCMI creates and disseminates Christian communication materials and services to people throughout the world.

How to Run the Alpha Course
by Nicky Gumbel

Published by David C. Cook Publishing Co. All rights reserved in North America.

Cover and interior illustrations by Charlie Mackesy
Cover Design by Cheryl Blum/Blum Graphic Design
Interior Design by Paula Grocke

ISBN 0-7814-5275-9

10 9 8 7 6 5 4 3 2 1

Table of Contents

Preface

I would like to express my thanks to Jon Soper who has acted as a researcher for this book and all the other *Alpha* resource books. I am so grateful for his thoroughness, speed, and efficiency as well as his very perceptive comments and suggestions.

I am grateful to all the people who have read the manuscripts and offered their valuable insights and criticisms. I want to thank especially Jo Glen, Patricia Hall, Helena Hird, Simon Levell, Ken Costa, Tamsen Carter, the Rev. Alex Welby, Judy Cahusac, Nicola Hinson, Chris Russell, and Simon Downham.

Finally, a big thank-you to Philippa Pearson Miles for her input on the administration of *Alpha* which has been incorporated into chapter 3. I thank Philippa also for typing the original manuscript (published in England as *Telling Others*) and organizing the project with her extraordinary combination of speed and enthusiasm, together with calmness and patience.

Nicky Gumbel

Foreword

As we look around at the state of the Church both in England and North America, the figures of declining congregations, the crumbling buildings, the general sense of failure that haunts so much of the Body of Jesus Christ today, there is a temptation for many of us involved in Christian ministry to feel discouraged. The apostle Paul faced the same situation, yet he was able to say, "Therefore, since through God's mercy we have this ministry, we do not lose heart" (2 Cor. 4:1).

It isn't that people are not interested in spirituality—interest in the occult, religious experiences, spiritism, and other related forms of alternative searches is as great today as ever it was—but the universal spiritual hunger, that need to fill the God-shaped hole, has not been met by those things. Our experience at Holy Trinity Brompton in London has been that people are now showing a new interest in the claims of Jesus Christ and the Christian faith. As our society moves into a post-Christian era many who are ignorant of the basic claimed truth of Christianity are wanting to find out more about Jesus of Nazareth, especially if they can be sure of an atmosphere of acceptance, without feeling threatened or judged or being made to look foolish. I think that is one of the reasons why the *Alpha Course* has proved to be such a success. The issues are clearly stated and the claims of Christ examined, all in the company of other searchers and in an atmosphere of love and acceptance.

Nicky Gumbel inherited *Alpha* several years ago and, since then, by taking account of literally thousands of questionnaires, has adapted and improved the course so it is truly molded to the perceived and experienced needs of those who attend. Without taking anything for granted, stripping the Gospel down to its bare essentials, he has made Christianity accessible to this generation.

But it is not simply hard work which has brought about the growth of *Alpha*. The touch of the Holy Spirit has brought the course to life from beginning to end. Hunger is created, in the hearts of those who are taking part, for the reality of God. The Spirit alone can satisfy them. By revealing the reality of the power of Jesus Christ to forgive, release, empower, and equip, new life begins for so many who are in need of God.

At the time of going to print, there are currently thousands of *Alpha Courses* running throughout England, North America, and other parts of the world. They range from small groups of five people to larger courses like one that is running here at Holy Trinity at the moment, with over five hundred people attending.

I know that you will find this book helpful. I am confident too that by God's grace you will find many people coming into the kingdom as a result of putting into practice the principles here.

Sandy Millar
Vicar of Holy Trinity Brompton
London, England

How to Use This Book

This book is based on the content *Telling Others* by Nicky Gumbel and sessions from an *Alpha Conference* (a regional informational and training seminar for those wanting to learn more about *Alpha*). The purpose of this book is to provide the background about the *Alpha Course,* including what it is it, how to set up and run a course, as well as the philosophy or heart of *Alpha.*

If you are an *Alpha* Leader or Director (or Administrator)—the one who is responsible for all details related to setting up and running an effective *Alpha Course*—this book is for you. We also recommend that every Small-Group Leader and Helper has a copy so they can see how they fit into the big picture and understand the philosophy of *Alpha.* It is also helpful for a church's entire staff and leadership team to have a chance to read this book. Since *Alpha* is an ongoing evangelism ministry, it is important that it has the support of the entire church.

There are three parts to this book.

Part I gives the history, theology, and vision behind *Alpha.* In this section you will:
• Read the history and background of *Alpha.*
• Learn how God is using *Alpha* worldwide to bring renewal and new life to people of all backgrounds.
• Master the basic terminology.
• Gain an understanding of the biblical foundation of the course.
    This portion of the book is helpful to read during the decision process concerning an *Alpha Course.* It is essential that everyone on the *Alpha* Team is exposed to the content of at least chapters 1 and 2.

Part II includes more of the nuts and bolts of setting up and running an *Alpha Course.* It includes the "how tos" and tips for success based on ministry at Holy Trinity Brompton Church (HTB) in London.
    The *Alpha* Leader will want to master this material in order to effectively communicate with others in the church and to train the Small-Group Leaders and Helpers and other members of the *Alpha* Team. The *Alpha* Director will need a copy to gain an understanding of the practical aspects of the course. The leaders and helpers will also benefit by having a copy to refer to throughout their training and during the course itself.

Part III includes dozens of reproducible resources to assist in the setting up and running of an *Alpha Course*. There are a detailed planning timeline, job descriptions for all *Alpha* Team positions, a complete listing of *Alpha* resources and related suggested reading, schedules for evening and daytime *Alpha Courses* and the weekend retreat, a sample press release and bulletin insert to help promote your local course, an *Alpha* Questionnaire, other miscellaneous forms, and the *Alpha* copyright statement included.

Part I

History, Theology, and Vision of
The Alpha Course

1
History

Thousands of people around the world are now taking part in *Alpha Courses*—a ten-week practical introduction to the Christian faith designed primarily for nonchurchgoers and those who have recently become Christians. In May 1993 we hosted a conference at Holy Trinity Brompton for church leaders who wanted to run such courses. Over a thousand people came, and hundreds of *Alpha Courses* began all over the UK as a result. Since then we have held a number of regional conferences and have also been invited to do some international conferences. The number of *Alpha Courses* in operation is growing daily.

Alpha has evolved from what was essentially a basic introduction for new Christians to something which is aimed primarily at those outside the church. *Alpha* began as a home group in 1976 in the living room of Charles Marnham, a clergyman at Holy Trinity Brompton Anglican Church (HTB), in England. Charles had a desire to reach others around him with the simple truths of the Christian faith. He began looking for a means of presenting the basic principles of the Christian faith to new Christians in a relaxed and informal setting. With this goal in mind, he devised the concept of the *Alpha Course.*

A few people gathered together in his living room each Wednesday evening for a light meal, a talk, and discussion groups. When Charles moved on, John Irvine took it over in 1981. He lengthened the course to ten weeks and added a weekend for teaching on the person and work of the Holy Spirit. When Nicky Lee took it over in 1985, there were about thirty-five people attending each of three annual courses and under his leadership that grew to well over a hundred. By the time I took over the *Alpha Course* in the early 1990s, *Alpha* was central to the church's life. Since then it has grown again to over five hundred people (including the leadership team) on each course (three a year).

During my second *Alpha Course* I made a discovery which transformed the church's approach to the course and later brought *Alpha* to the attention of churches throughout the UK. As I looked around at the 13 members of my small group, I was surprised that besides the three Christian helpers, all other members were nonchurchgoers.

It was astonishing. This group of 10 raised all the normal objections:

There are numerous stories of people finding faith . . . through *Alpha.*

"What about other religions?" "What about suffering?" and so on. We had a stormy first six weeks, but the entire group went on the weekend away.

At the weekend retreat, which focuses on the person and work of the Holy Spirit, all 10 announced their Christian conversion. When we came back from the weekend retreat, we had the most amazing evening listening to all their testimonies.

This experience transformed my thinking about *Alpha.* I realized how this simple course in basic Christianity could become a powerful tool for evangelism.

Adjustments were made in the method of welcome, the atmosphere of the small groups, the food, the seating, the flowers, the sound, and the content of the actual talks. We emphasized that everyone should be allowed to ask any question they liked in their small groups. Nothing should be treated as too trivial, threatening, or illogical. Every question would be addressed courteously and thoughtfully. It also became a policy that the people were given the freedom to return or not. No one was going to chase them. The course grew quickly—so quickly that the location had to be changed and the *Alpha* Team of helpers massively increased.

CHANGED LIVES

There are numerous stories of people finding faith in Christ through *Alpha.* One example is Lee Duckett, a telecommunications engineer who arrived to repair the phones at HTB one morning in 1993. He started talking with the receptionist who suggested he try *Alpha.*

He came the first night and said later, "I couldn't believe it. It wasn't what I expected. All the people looked normal." He was impressed by the leader of his small group. "I thought, 'He's got what I'm missing. He's got something. Something I want.' "

During that course, Lee gave his life to Jesus Christ and later commented, "My life has completely changed. I now look at the world through different eyes. I feel love for everyone and an inner peace that I never imagined could exist."

Lee is just one of hundreds of others who have become Christians through the *Alpha* ministry at HTB. Many have completed questionnaires at the end of the course and have written how their lives have been transformed.

One wrote, "I feel I've walked through the back of the cupboard, like C.S. Lewis's children in *The Lion, the Witch and the Wardrobe.* I am gazing eagerly around with so much to learn about the new world I find myself in."

GROWTH OF ALPHA

Since that second course of my involvement, the course has been steadily growing. The growth comes through friends. At the end of each course there is a Celebration Dinner which now attracts around 1,000 people. This is one of the key events for bringing people to the next course. People who are converted on *Alpha* have a circle of people to bring to the dinner and invite on the next course. People often bring their family and friends to the next *Alpha*, and that is how it grows.

The growth comes through friends.

One young man came and then he brought his parents, who are now leaders on the course. Then he brought his girlfriend, who also became a Christian. It's all friendship-based. There's no knocking on doors. There's little advertising. It's simply friends bringing friends.

This same model is now being used effectively in over 5000 courses worldwide. An estimated 120,000 people are involved with an *Alpha Course* somewhere in the world each week. This includes the *Alpha* Team (those who host and run *Alpha*) and the guests who are searching for answers to the questions of life. Churches of almost every Christian denomination including, but not limited to, Anglican, Assemblies of God, Baptist, Christian Missionary Alliance, Congregational, Episcopal, Lutheran, Methodist, Pentecostal, Presbyterian, Roman Catholic, United Church of Christ, and Vineyard Fellowship are running *Alpha*. Independent and non-denominational churches also hold *Alpha Courses*.

The growth of *Alpha* worldwide has been very encouraging. Attendance has grown from a total of about 500 people in four courses during 1991 to an estimated attendance of more than 500,000 in 1997. There are over 5000 courses worldwide with about 20 new courses outside the UK registering each week. In addition, there are many courses that do not register with the international office in London. Courses are now running in about 50 countries in addition to England, Canada, and the United States. The table below shows estimated attendance at *Alpha Courses* from 1991–1997.

Year	Courses	People
1991	4	500
1992	5	1,000
1993	200	4,500
1994	750	30,000
1995	2,500	100,000
1996	5,000	250,000
1997		500,000

"The most encouraging thing is that it is God at work."

ALPHA IN NORTH AMERICA

Across North America lives are being touched by God's love through the ministry of the Holy Spirit. Churches that host an *Alpha Course* or an *Alpha* Conference are encouraged as they see the impact on their congregations and communities.

Following an *Alpha* Conference in Toronto, Ted Ward, chair of the evangelism group of the host church, said, "With 700 delegates, 90 volunteers, 150 churches, and 25 denominations represented, we see this as the largest conference on evangelism ever held by Canadian Anglicans. The most encouraging thing is that it is God at work. It has to be, otherwise you wouldn't see this kind of snowballing effect."[1]

According to *Alpha News:*

> Hillary Bercovici has been involved in three courses in a small church in Westchester, New York, after attending the *Alpha* Conference in Washington, D.C., in 1995. He said, "We were encouraged to take a cookie-cutter approach—to do exactly what the book said—and we did. We followed it to a T and found that all the little things matched exactly. So following the recipe exactly was the thing that was so helpful.
>
> "In the first course we had around 40 people. The second was very small with four participants and five leaders. The next course was around 38 and in that course we hit the fringe of the church and at the *Alpha* Dinner we had 65. So we are now looking forward to a course that will be over two-thirds outsiders."[2]

According to Justin Dennison, senior pastor of Bramalea Baptist Church near Toronto, *Alpha* has "made a bridge between those on the fringe of faith with those who are deeply involved. [I'm] amazed at the people who come and the friends they invite. Nothing has impacted our church at a greater level than this."[3]

Elaine Young, wife of the rector of Bridgetown, Nova Scotia, wrote the following:

> *Alpha* has become a household word in . . . Bridgetown, a rural community nestled in the Annapolis Valley of Nova Scotia with a population of approximately 1,000.
>
> It all began when a parishioner read about *Alpha* in an English newspaper. Several generous donations allowed our parish to begin the leadership training course. Eight people from our own Christian community and the

surrounding area linked up with Anglicans from several parishes for a series of evening potluck meals.

As the weeks unfolded, we all became more comfortable with each other. It was exciting to watch the level of faith rise in the group. . . . In reflection, we would say that it has been a wonderful, positive experience for our parish and community. Nearly all our participants would say *Alpha* enabled them to take a step forward in their relationship with God.

The spiritual impact of *Alpha* upon our community has been significant. We expect that it will prove to be an integral part of the renewal that God has begun in our parish. But the success of this program lies not in itself. By revealing the reality of the power of Jesus Christ to forgive, to release, empower, and equip, new life begins for so many who are in need of God.[4]

 "Alpha has given us a model for effective evangelism."

Ed Wright, a pastor from Columbus, Ohio, reported at an *Alpha* Conference in Nashville that many people were converted, some dramatically, on the first *Alpha Course* in his church.[5] He had heard about *Alpha* at a meeting in Florida and wanted to know more. So he ordered some resources. Because he first wanted to learn how to run *Alpha*, he decided to keep the numbers down by telling people that if they wanted to come, they had to bring someone with them who was unchurched or unsaved. There were about 75 the first night and about 40 completed the course. Pastor Wright said, "I wanted unsaved people there because I needed to know it really worked. It does!"

The members of his small group were all between 18 and 25 years old. They wore baggy, grungy clothes and had jet black hair, black fingernails, tattoos, and body piercing—not typical of his church! The young people were so suspicious and skeptical—the first weeks made no impact on them at all. But it was the developing relationships that hooked them and kept them coming back. What really did it for them was the session on the Holy Spirit. After the talk Pastor Wright told them that the Ministry Team was going to pray for them. One person was overwhelmed by the Spirit, and the young people in the pastor's group just started looking at each other, saying, "Did you feel that?" They sensed the presence of the Holy Spirit before they were even saved or had an awareness of Christ in their lives. Two of the young men came back to church where the pastor prayed with them and led them to Christ.

He reports, "*Alpha* has given us a model for effective evangelism.

Relationships are formed on *Alpha* and unchurched participants are loved even before they are saved."

TERMINOLOGY

As *Alpha* has grown throughout the UK and now internationally, it seemed sensible to pass on some of the things we have learned over the years. Therefore we have developed *Alpha* Conferences and a variety of print, video, and audio resources. Historically we have found the easiest way to learn how to "do *Alpha*" is to hear from others who are running effective courses. There are two major areas of *Alpha:* setting up the course and running the course.

SETTING UP THE ALPHA COURSE

The first way to learn about how to get *Alpha* started is to attend an *Alpha* Conference. Regional training sessions are held on the principles, philosophy, and practicalities of the *Alpha Course.* Churches have found it helpful to send their leadership teams to these conferences to capture the vision of *Alpha* and to gain an understanding of the basic "how tos." (See page 59 for more information on *Alpha* Conferences.)

There are also a number of helpful resources that can be used to share the vision of *Alpha* with others in the church and to train the *Alpha* Team. These resources include:

Title	Description
• The *Alpha Course* Introductory Video	Fifteen-minute overview of *Alpha*
• How to Run the *Alpha Course:* A Handbook for *Alpha* Directors, Leaders, and Helpers	The *Alpha* Conference in book form
• *Alpha* Conference Tapes	Twelve audiotapes of an entire *Alpha* Conference
• How to Run *Alpha* Video	Two video sessions on the Principles and Practicalities of *Alpha*
• *Alpha* Leaders Training Tapes OR *Alpha* Leaders Training Video	Three training sessions on Leading Small Groups, Pastoral Care, and Ministry
• The *Alpha Course* Leader's Guide	Part I is used to train the Small-Group Leaders and Helpers

See the table entitled "The *Alpha* Conference" on page 155 in Appendix G for an explanation of how the content of these resources correlates.

RUNNING THE ALPHA COURSE

A variety of materials have been developed to assist local churches and individuals in implementing an *Alpha Course*. Following are a listing and brief description of each resource.

Title	Description
• Registration Brochures (packs of 50)	4-color, ready to customize
• *Questions of Life*	The *Alpha Course* in book form
• The *Alpha Course* Tapes OR	Includes all 15 talks
• The *Alpha Course* Video	5-video set including 15 talks
• *Why Jesus?* or *Why Christmas?*	Presentation of the Gospel
• The *Alpha Course* Manual	Talk outlines and room for notetaking for each participant and for Small-Group Leader and Helper
• The *Alpha Course* Leader's Guide	Part II includes suggestions for group discussions and Bible studies for Small-Group Leaders and Helpers
• *Searching Issues*	Biblical help with key objections to Christianity

The table on page 157 shows how these resources correlate with each other.

2
Principles

When I came to you, brothers, I did not come with eloquence or superior wisdom as I proclaimed to you the testimony about God. For I resolved to know nothing while I was with you except Jesus Christ and him crucified. I came to you in weakness and fear, and with much trembling. My message and my preaching were not with wise and persuasive words, but with a demonstration of the Spirit's power, so that your faith might not rest on men's wisdom, but on God's power. —1 Corinthians 2:1-5

I have never been a natural evangelist. I have never found it easy to talk to my friends about Jesus Christ. Some people are completely natural evangelists: they find it the easiest thing in the world.

I recently heard about one man who seizes every opportunity to talk to people about Jesus. If he is standing at a bus stop and the bus is late, he turns that situation into a conversation about the Second Coming!

I have another friend who is a tremendously confident evangelist and speaks about Jesus wherever he goes. On a train he will speak to the person seated opposite about Jesus. If he is walking along the street, he will turn to someone and get into conversation with them about Jesus. When he and his family go to a family restaurant, upon finishing his meal, he bangs the table and calls for silence in the restaurant. He then stands up and preaches the Gospel for five minutes. He says that at the end people come up to him and say, "Thank you very much; that was very helpful." Now I couldn't do that!

When I first became a Christian, I was so excited about what had happened that I longed for everybody to follow suit. After I had been a Christian for only a few days I went to a party, determined to tell everyone. I saw a friend dancing and decided the first step was to make her realize her need for Jesus. So I went up to her and said, "You look awful. You really need Jesus." She thought I had gone mad. It was not the most effective way of telling someone the Good News. (However, she did later become a Christian, quite independently of me, and she is now my wife!)

If we charge around like a bull in a china shop, sooner or later we get hurt. Even if we approach the subject sensitively, we may still get hurt. When we do, we tend to withdraw. Certainly this was my experience. After

> **!** *Alpha* is
> evangelism for
> ordinary people.

a few years, I moved from the danger of insensitivity and fell into the opposite danger of fear.

There was a time (ironically, when I was in seminary) when I became fearful of even talking about Jesus to those who were not Christians. On one occasion, a group of us from college went to a parish mission on the outskirts of Liverpool to tell people the Good News. Each night we had supper with different people from the parish. One night my friend Rupert and I were sent to a couple who were on the fringe of the church. To be more accurate, the wife was on the fringe and the husband was not a churchgoer. Halfway through the main course the husband asked me what we were doing up there. I stumbled, stammered, hesitated, and prevaricated. He kept repeating the question. Eventually Rupert said straight out, "We have come here to tell people about Jesus." I felt deeply embarrassed and hoped the ground would swallow us all up! I realized how frozen with fear I had become and that I was afraid to even take the name of Jesus on my lips.

Ever since then I've been looking for ways in which ordinary people like me, who aren't naturally gifted evangelists, can communicate their faith with friends, family, and colleagues without feeling fearful or risking insensitivity. I have found that *Alpha* is evangelism for ordinary people.

Recent surveys have shown that approximately 1,000 people left the Church of England every week during the decade 1980 to 1990. Other denominations suffered a similar decline. The vast majority of the population of the United Kingdom do not attend church, and of those who do, many only go at Christmas or Easter. Following in the wake of the decline in Christian belief, there has been a decline in the moral climate. The fabric of our society is unraveling. Every day in Britain at least 480 couples are divorced, 170 babies are born to teenage mothers, and 470 babies are aborted. In addition, at least one new crime is committed every six seconds and a violent attack takes place every two minutes. Although there are 30,000 Christian clergy of all types, there are more than 80,000 registered witches and fortune tellers.[1]

But at the same time, shoots of new life are springing up all over the place. New churches are being planted and many churches are seeing growth, sometimes slow and sometimes quite dramatic. There are new Christian initiatives arising out of the renewal movement in the Decade of Evangelism. One of those new shoots is the *Alpha Course*. All of us involved with it have sensed the extraordinary blessing of God upon it.

I realize that we need to be cautious about saying this is a work of God. I know the story of the man who came up to a preacher and said, "That was a great talk." The preacher rather piously replied, "It wasn't me, it was the Lord," to which the man replied, "It wasn't that good!" In saying that we believe *Alpha* is a work of God I am not for a moment suggesting that it is perfect. I'm sure that it is greatly marred by human error and frailty. There is much room for improvement and we try to listen carefully to constructive criticism. Nor do we believe that it is the only method of evangelism that God is blessing: far from it. Nevertheless, all the signs point to it being an extraordinary work of God and we are deeply grateful.

When *Alpha* first started growing, I thought, "How could something that started in Central London work elsewhere?" *Alpha* currently runs in dozens of countries, including Zimbabwe, Kenya, Norway, Denmark, Sweden, Germany, Malaysia, Hong Kong, Australia, New Zealand, United States, Canada, and many more.

While running an *Alpha* Conference in Zimbabwe, I discovered that *Alpha* was not only running among the English-speaking white Zimbabweans but also among the Shona-speaking people in their own language. Zimbabwe has a population of just over 10 million people: there are 80,000 whites in Zimbabwe but 90 percent of the black population speak Shona. While I was at the conference, I met a man called Edward Ngamuda. He had done *Alpha* originally in English but then thought that he would like to run the course in Shona. A couple who had come to Christ on *Alpha* asked him to come and run the course with the 900 people who worked on their farm. Thirty people came on the first course and 50 came on the second. I asked him whether these people were Christians when they came on the course. "No," he replied, "we had a Muslim, a witch doctor, and a polygamist come." I asked how the polygamist happened to be there and was told that his first wife came on the first course and that she had brought him and the other two wives on the next one! Edward assured me that *Alpha* worked better in Shona than it did in English. It was then that I began to realize that this course, which started in London, could operate in different countries and cultures.

Why is this? I believe it is because the *Alpha Course* is based on six New Testament principles. In this chapter, I want to look at each of these principles in turn.

PRINCIPLE 1: EVANGELISM[2] IS MOST EFFECTIVE THROUGH THE LOCAL CHURCH

John Stott, author of many books and Rector Emeritus of All Souls, Langham Place in England, has described evangelism through the local church as "the most normal, natural and productive method of spreading the Gospel today."[3] Of course, other forms of evangelism work too. Missions and Billy Graham-style crusades clearly have been greatly used by

God. They raise the profile of the church and are still effective means of bringing people to Christ. In our church we often take teams on outreaches to universities and elsewhere and we appreciate the value and fruitfulness of this type of evangelism. But missions are more likely to bear lasting fruit if they are based in an ongoing program of local church evangelism, which has the great advantage of continuity of relationships.

WHAT YOU SEE IS WHAT YOU GET

Someone may respond at a crusade or mission and be referred to their local church. They may be disappointed to find the environment of the church radically different from the meeting which attracted them in the first place and so they subsequently stop attending. This is one of the reasons that follow-up after big crusades is so hard. By contrast, if someone is introduced to Christianity at their local church, they become familiar with the place and the people, and are therefore much more likely to stay.

MOBILIZES A WHOLE ARMY OF EVANGELISTS

Evangelism through the local church involves not just one great evangelist, or even an evangelist in a team, but a whole army of evangelists. On every one of our *Alpha Courses* at Holy Trinity Brompton in London, we have at least 120 people involved in evangelism. Throughout a whole year perhaps 250 different people are involved. This is excellent training for these people and taps into a resource which might otherwise have remained dormant in the church.

A recent Gallup survey in the USA claimed that only 10 percent of church members are active in any form of personal ministry, but that 40 percent have expressed an interest. *Alpha* is one way of mobilizing these people. Reports coming back from churches time and again speak of the effect *Alpha* has had on their church. People are excited to see new people coming to Christ, to welcome them into their congregation, and to see their own part in this process.

FRIENDSHIP-BASED

If someone comes to Christ on the course and is filled with the Spirit, they will naturally tell their friends, family, and colleagues. They will say to them, "Come and see! Come to the next course!" Then many more people come to the next course and they all have circles of friends which get penetrated. This is a New Testament model of evangelism: Peter brought his brother Andrew; Philip brought his friend Nathaniel; the woman at the

Alpha is one way of mobilizing people.

well went back and told everyone in her town; and Matthew the tax collector threw a party and invited all his work colleagues to meet Jesus. This is the way *Alpha* works.

One crusade may bring great blessing, but it is limited both in time and space. If every local church in the world were running an effective ongoing program of local church evangelism and every month people were coming to Christ and bringing their friends and these friends bringing other friends—imagine how quickly the world would be reached for Christ!

Michael Green, Advisor in Evangelism to the Archbishops of Canterbury and York, in his book *Evangelism through the Local Church*, summed up the need for this kind of evangelism:

> Whenever Christianity has been at its most healthy, evangelism has stemmed from the local church, and has had a noticeable impact on the surrounding area. I do not believe that the re-Christianization of the West can take place without the renewal of local churches in this whole area of evangelism. We need a thoughtful, sustained, relevant presentation of the Christian faith, in word and in action, embodied in a warm, prayerful, lively local church which has a real concern for its community at all levels. . . . Such evangelism, in and from the local church, is not only much needed but . . . eminently possible. I believe it to be the most natural, long-lasting and effective evangelism that is open to us. If local churches were engaging in loving, outgoing evangelism within their neighborhoods, many of our evangelistic campaigns, missions and crusades would be rendered much less necessary.[4]

THE MORE CHECKOUTS, THE MORE CUSTOMERS

This is a principle of the supermarket that we learned from the Americans. The more churches running *Alpha* or another evangelism program, the more people who will be reached by Christ. Suppose that out of the 300,000+ churches in America and the 28,000 in Canada every one was running an effective program of evangelism week in and week out, month in and month out, and year in and year out. Imagine how quickly the continent could be reached for Christ.

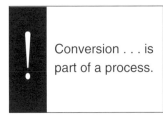

Conversion . . . is part of a process.

PRINCIPLE 2: EVANGELISM IS A PROCESS

New Testament expressions

Conversion may take place in a moment but it is part of a process. All New Testament expressions of conversion are process words. Jesus used the expression "born again" (John 3:3) for the beginning of a spiritual life, and the New Testament speaks about becoming a child of God. While the birth of a child may be a onetime event, there is a much longer process before and afterward. The Bible uses many other images to represent spiritual growth: some are taken from agriculture, others from the ideas of building or traveling. All these involve a process.

Alpha is a ten-week course involving a total of 15 talks which include a weekend retreat and a Celebration Dinner at the end. We do not expect people to respond to the Gospel after the first week (although some do). We recognize that people need time to think, watch, listen, and talk through their questions and difficulties. Each person is beginning at a different stage.

Some are already Christians but will often say, in retrospect, that at the start of the course they were Christians "without any real experience of God." Others are at the point of new birth when they begin *Alpha*. Some have already given their lives to Christ at the Celebration Dinner at the end of the previous course, others at a guest service before the beginning of *Alpha*. Still others perhaps come to faith through the witness of their family or a friend. Many are still a long way off when they begin *Alpha*. Some are convinced atheists, some are New Agers, some are adherents to other religions or cults. Many are living in lifestyles which are far from Christian. Some are alcoholics, others are compulsive gamblers, many are living with partners to whom they are not married, and some are in a homosexual lifestyle. We welcome them all. Some will complete the whole course and still not be Christians at the end; we hope they will be unable to say they have not heard the Gospel. Others will give their lives to Christ somewhere on the course. For nearly all of them, *Alpha* will enable them to take a step forward in their relationship with God.

Process operates at two levels

Gradually seeing the picture

First is the level of understanding. The fact there is a process of evangelism spread over 15 sessions enables us to give more attention to aspects of the Christian faith than one would be able to in one evangelistic talk. For example, in 1994 I saw a man named Guy standing at the back of the room who looked very uncomfortable and worried. When I introduced myself, he said, "I don't want to be here, I've been dragged along." I said, "Great! Let me introduce you to 11 other people who don't want to be here," and I took him to meet my small group. At the end of the evening I heard Guy talking to someone else in the group. "Are you coming back next week?" he asked. The other man replied, "Yes, I'll be here." To which Guy said, "Well, if you're coming back next week, I'll come back next week." Six weeks later he said to me, "This course is like a jigsaw puzzle. Every time I come back another piece fits into place. And I'm beginning to get the picture."

> **!** We believe that Christianity is based in history.

Building trust

Furthermore, the fact that *Alpha* is a process enables trust to develop. This is the second level. There is a great deal of cynicism, skepticism, and distrust about the Christian church. I had no idea of the extent of this until I spoke to someone who said that for the first three weeks of the course he had not eaten the food in case it was drugged. That was an extreme case of distrust, but many people wonder if the church is after their money, their mind, or something else. It can take a few weeks for a level of trust to build. As the guests get to know their Small-Group Leaders, they begin to see that the *Alpha* Team is not "after" anything and they start to listen.

PRINCIPLE 3: EVANGELISM INVOLVES THE WHOLE PERSON

Evangelism involves an appeal to the whole person: mind, heart, and will. Each talk is designed to appeal to all three, although in some of the talks the emphasis will be on just one.

APPEAL TO THE HEAD

We appeal to the mind because we believe that Christianity is based in history: on the life, death, and resurrection of Jesus Christ. We preach "Jesus Christ and him crucified" (1 Cor. 2:2). We seek to persuade with every argument we can muster, just as Paul did on so many occasions (for example, Acts 18:4). We try to teach only what we can establish from the Bible and we point people to the biblical text. We do not expect anyone to take a "blind leap" of faith. Rather, we hope they will take a reasonable step of faith based on reasonable grounds.

APPEAL TO THE HEART

The Gospel involves both the rational and the experiential.

Secondly, we appeal to the heart. Our message does not simply require an assent of the intellect to a series of propositions, rather it calls people to a love-relationship with Jesus Christ. John Stott has written:

> There is a place for emotion in spiritual experience. The Holy Spirit's . . . ministry is not limited to illuminating our minds and teaching us about Christ. He also pours God's love into our hearts. Similarly, he bears witness with our spirit that we are God's children, for he causes us to say "Abba, Father" and to exclaim with gratitude, "How great is the love the Father has lavished on us, that we should be called children of God!" . . . I think it was Bishop Handley Moule at the end of the last century who gave this good advice: "Beware equally of an undevotional theology (i.e., mind without heart) and of an untheological devotion (i.e., heart without mind)."[5]

Graham Cray, principal of Ridley Hall Theological College in Cambridge, has spoken with great insight about the culture of the 1990s, which is in the process of shifting from an Enlightenment culture to a new and coming one. In the Enlightenment, reason reigned supreme and explanation led to experience. In the present transitional culture with its "pick-and-mix" worldview, in which the New Age movement is a potent strand, experiences lead to explanation.

I have found during *Alpha* that those from an essentially Enlightenment background feel at home with the parts of the course which appeal to the mind, but often have difficulty in experiencing the Holy Spirit. Others coming from the New Age movement find that rational and historical explanations leave them cold, but at the weekend away they are on more familiar territory in experiencing the Spirit. Previously they will have been seeking experiences which have then left them discontented and only in experiencing a relationship with God through Jesus Christ do they find their hunger is satisfied.

The Gospel involves both the rational and the experiential and it impacts both those from an Enlightenment background who need to experience God and those who have sought experiences but who need to understand the truth about God.

APPEAL TO THE WILL

Thirdly, we seek to appeal to the will. We recognize, of course, that no one can come to the Father unless God calls them. As Jesus said, "No one knows the Son except the Father, and no one knows the Father except the Son and those to whom the Son chooses to reveal him" (Matt. 11:27). On the other hand, Jesus went on to say in the very next verse, "Come to me, all you who are weary and burdened, and I will give you rest" (vs. 28). In other words, He called for a decision.

There is a difference between an appeal to the will and the wrong form of pressure. We try to avoid all forms of pressure on *Alpha*. We do not endlessly exhort anyone to respond or chase after people if they do not come back: it is up to them to decide. Over the period of 10 weeks, as we pray and allow the Holy Spirit to do His work, giving people the opportunity to respond, we are, in effect, making a continuous appeal to their wills.

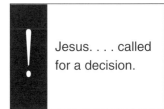

Jesus. . . . called for a decision.

PRINCIPLE 4: MODELS OF EVANGELISM IN THE NEW TESTAMENT INCLUDE CLASSICAL, HOLISTIC, AND POWER EVANGELISM

Graham Tomlin, lecturer at Wycliffe Hall Theological College, Oxford, draws attention to three different models of evangelism.[6] Clearly these three are not mutually exclusive and we very much hope that the *Alpha Course* involves all three models.

CLASSICAL EVANGELISM (WORDS)

First, there is what he calls classical evangelism which involves "the proclamation of the unchanging message." Certainly, at the heart of *Alpha* is the proclamation of the Gospel of Jesus Christ: the first talk is about Christ's deity, the second is about His death on the cross for us, and each talk has at its core some principle of Christian belief and living.

HOLISTIC EVANGELISM (WORKS)

Second, there is holistic evangelism. As John Stott wrote, "We are convinced that God has given us social as well as evangelistic responsibilities in his world."[7] Evangelism and social action go hand in hand. The latter involves both social justice in the removal of injustice, inhumanity, and inequality, and social service in relieving human need, such as hunger, homelessness, and poverty. We attempt during *Alpha* to avoid the dangers of pietism or super spiritualism by our teaching and example, believing that evangelism is fundamentally linked to social responsibility.

The central theme in the teaching of Jesus is the kingdom of God.

POWER EVANGELISM (WONDERS)

Third, there is power evangelism, where the proclamation of the Gospel goes hand in hand with a demonstration of the Spirit's power (for example, 1 Corinthians 2:1-5). We include this third element because we believe it is firmly based in New Testament practice.

It used to be argued that you cannot take doctrine from narrative, but New Testament scholars have shown to the satisfaction of theologians of all varieties that the Gospel writers were not only historians, they were theologians as well. In a different literary form, they were writing theology as much as Paul or the other writers of the New Testament Epistles. In the Gospels, the central theme in the teaching of Jesus is the kingdom of God.[8] The coming of the Kingdom involved not only the spoken proclamation of the Gospel but also a visible demonstration of its presence by signs, wonders, and miracles. Each of the Gospel writers expected these to continue.

We can see this from the way in which Matthew sets out his Gospel. He tells us that "Jesus went throughout Galilee, teaching in their synagogues, preaching the good news of the kingdom, and healing every disease and sickness among the people" (Matt. 4:23). He then gives some of the teaching and preaching of Jesus in chapters 5-7 (the Sermon on the Mount), then nine miracles (mainly of healing), and he concludes with an almost exact repetition of Matthew 4:23: "Jesus went through all the towns and villages, teaching in their synagogues, preaching the good news of the kingdom and healing every disease and sickness" (Matt. 9:35). Matthew is using a literary device of repetition known as an *inclusio,* a short piece of text which appears at the beginning and at the end of a particular section and acts as punctuation by enclosing a theme. Having shown what Jesus Himself did, Matthew tells us that Jesus then sent the Twelve out to do the same. He told them to go out and preach the same message: " 'The kingdom of heaven is near.' Heal the sick, raise the dead, cleanse those who have leprosy, drive out demons. . . ." (Matt. 10:7-8).

At the end of his Gospel, Matthew makes it clear that Jesus expected all His disciples to "go and make disciples of all nations . . . teaching them to obey *everything* I have commanded you" (Matt. 28:19-20; italics mine). This surely includes not only His ethical teaching, but also the earlier commissions.

In Mark's Gospel we see a similar pattern. Mark tells us that Jesus proclaimed the Good News (Mark 1:14 onwards), demonstrating it by signs and wonders (Mark 1:21 onwards). The kingdom of God was inaugurated by Jesus and is still growing to this day. There is no reason why its fundamental nature should have changed. Indeed, in the longer ending of Mark (which is, at the very least, good evidence of what the early church believed Jesus' commission to be), Jesus said, " 'Go into all the world and preach the good news to all creation . . . and these signs will accompany those who believe: In my name they will drive out demons . . . they will place their hands on sick people, and they will get well. . . .' Then the disciples went out and preached everywhere, and the Lord worked with them and confirmed his word by the signs that accompanied it" (Mark 16:15-20; italics mine). Jesus says, " . . . these signs will accompany those *who believe*"—that is to say, those who believe in Jesus Christ, which means all Christians.

"Anyone who has faith in me will do what I have been doing."

For Luke's theology we need to look at both Luke and Acts. Luke tells us in his Gospel: "When Jesus had called the Twelve together, he gave them power and authority to drive out all demons and to cure diseases, and he sent them out to preach the kingdom of God and to heal the sick" (Luke 9:1-2). Nor was it only the Twelve to whom He gave this commission; He also appointed 72 others and told them to go out and "heal the sick who are there and tell them, 'The kingdom of God is near you' " (Luke 10:9).

In the Book of Acts this continues beyond the time Jesus was on earth. After the outpouring of the Holy Spirit, there is a remarkable continuation of supernatural power, ranging from speaking in tongues to raising the dead. These demonstrations of power continue right through to the last chapter (Acts 28:7-9). Throughout Acts we see the outworking of this commission. The disciples continued to preach and teach, but also to heal the sick, raise the dead, and cast out demons (Acts 3:1-10; 4:12; 5:12-16; 8:5-13; 9:32-43; 14:3, 8-10; 19:11-12; 20:9-12; 28:8-9).

Nor is this ministry in the Spirit's power confined to the Synoptic Gospels. In John's Gospel Jesus is reported to have said, in the context of miracles, "Anyone who has faith in me will do what I have been doing. He will do even greater things than these, because I am going to the Father" (John 14:12). Clearly no one has performed miracles of greater quality than Jesus, but there has been a greater quantity since Jesus returned to the Father. He has not ceased to perform miracles, but now He uses weak and imperfect human beings. Again it says, "Anyone who has faith in me": that is, all Christians. These commands and promises are not restricted anywhere to a special category of people.

Signs and miracles were a central part of Paul's proclamation of the Gospel (Rom. 15:19). It is also clear from 1 Corinthians 12-14 that Paul did not believe that such abilities were confined to the apostles and he expected the more obviously supernatural gifts of the Spirit to continue in an effective and healthy church. He speaks about "gifts of healing," "miraculous powers," "prophecy," "speaking in different kinds of tongues,"

We do not draw ultimate attention to the signs and wonders.

and "the interpretation of tongues." He described these as being given to different members of the Body of Christ and as being the work of the Spirit (1 Cor. 12:7-11).

Nowhere in the New Testament does it say that these gifts will cease at the end of the apostolic age. On the contrary, Paul says that they will only cease when "perfection comes" (1 Cor. 13:10). Some have identified "perfection" here with the formation of the canon of Scripture, saying that as we now have the Bible, we have no need of "imperfect" spiritual gifts. However, the context for this verse clearly shows that Paul is identifying "perfection" with the return of Jesus. The world is not yet perfect, neither do we see Jesus "face to face" (vs. 12), nor do we "know fully" (vs. 12) but we know only "in part" (vs. 12). This "perfection" will only occur when Jesus returns and then these gifts will no longer be necessary. Until that moment they are a vital part of the church's armory. Indeed, this passage shows that Paul did not expect the gifts to cease until the return of Jesus.

Likewise, the writer to the Hebrews says that God testified to His message by "signs, wonders and various miracles, and gifts of the Holy Spirit" (Heb 2:4). Nowhere in the Bible is the supernatural display of the power of the Holy Spirit confined to any particular period of history. On the contrary, such signs, wonders, and miracles are part of the Kingdom which was inaugurated by Jesus Christ and continues to this day. Hence we should expect today to see the supernatural display of the power of the Holy Spirit as part of His kingdom activity and as an authentication of the Good News. However, we do not draw ultimate attention to the signs and wonders, but to the God of love who performs them.

PRINCIPLE 5: EVANGELISM IN THE POWER OF THE HOLY SPIRIT IS BOTH DYNAMIC AND EFFECTIVE

On the Day of Pentecost Peter preached with such power that the people were "cut to the heart" and 3000 were converted (Acts 2:37-41). The remarkable events continued: "Everyone was filled with awe, and many wonders and miraculous signs were done by the apostles. . . . And the Lord added to their number daily those who were being saved" (vss. 43-47).

Remarkable healings followed (e.g., Acts 3:1-10). People were astonished and came running to find out what had happened (vs. 11). Peter and John preached the Gospel with great boldness: "When they saw the courage of Peter and John and realized that they were unschooled, ordinary men, they were astonished and they took note that these men had been with Jesus. But since they could see the man who had been healed standing there with them, there was nothing they could say" (Acts

4:13-14). The authorities had no idea what to do because "all the people were praising God for what had happened. For the man who was miraculously healed was over forty years old" (vss. 21-22).

The dynamic effect on the crowds continued:

> The apostles performed many miraculous signs and wonders among the people. And all the believers used to meet together in Solomon's Colonnade. No one else dared join them, even though they were highly regarded by the people. Nevertheless, more and more men and women believed in the Lord and were added to their number. As a result, people brought the sick into the streets and laid them on beds and mats so that at least Peter's shadow might fall on some of them as he passed by. Crowds gathered also from the towns around Jerusalem, bringing their sick and those tormented by evil spirits, and all of them were healed (Acts 5:12-16).

People continued to be converted. "So the word of God spread. The number of disciples in Jerusalem increased rapidly, and a large number of priests became obedient to the faith" (Acts 6:7). As we go on in the Book of Acts the same pattern continues. When Paul and Barnabas went to Iconium, "they spoke so effectively that a great number of Jews and Gentiles believed" (Acts 14:1). They spent a considerable time there "speaking boldly for the Lord, who confirmed the message of his grace by enabling them to do miraculous signs and wonders" (vs. 3). In Lystra a crippled man was healed (vs. 8). In Derbe "they preached the good news in that city and won a large number of disciples" (vs. 21).

Later on, Luke tells us what happened to 12 Ephesian men: "When Paul placed his hands on them, the Holy Spirit came on them, and they spoke in tongues and prophesied" (Acts 19:6). Further, in Ephesus, "God did extraordinary miracles through Paul, so that even handkerchiefs and aprons that had touched him were taken to the sick, and their illnesses were cured and the evil spirits left them" (vss. 11-12).

Far from dwindling away through the period covered by the Book of Acts, this spiritual dynamic continued. Even in the last chapter we read of Paul praying for Publius's father: "His father was sick in bed, suffering from fever and dysentery. Paul went in to see him and, after prayer, placed his hands on him and healed him. When this had happened, the rest of the sick on the island came and were cured" (Acts 28:8-9). All the way through Acts we see the dynamic effect of the coming of the kingdom of God accompanied by conversions, miraculous signs, healings, visions, tongues, prophecy, raising the dead, and casting out evil spirits.

The same God is at work today among us. Evangelism can still be dynamic and effective. We are finding this to be the case on the *Alpha Course*, not only at HTB but all over the country and in different parts of the world.

PRINCIPLE 6: EFFECTIVE EVANGELISM REQUIRES THE FILLING AND REFILLING OF THE SPIRIT

Jesus told His disciples, "You will receive power when the Holy Spirit comes on you; and you will be my witnesses in Jerusalem, and in all Judea and Samaria, and to the ends of the earth" (Acts 1:8). On the Day of Pentecost the promise of Jesus was fulfilled and "all of them were filled with the Holy Spirit and began to speak in other tongues as the Spirit enabled them" (Acts 2:4).

However, it did not end there. Later on we read of Peter being "filled with the Holy Spirit" again (Acts 4:8). Still later the disciples (including Peter) were filled again (Acts 4:31). The filling of the Holy Spirit is not a onetime experience. Paul urges the Christians of Ephesus to "be filled with the Spirit" (Eph 5:18) and the emphasis is on continuing to be filled.

Professor Wayne Grudem writes the most useful chapter I know of on this subject in his masterful *Systematic Theology.*[9] Sometimes people use the analogy of a glass of water for people being filled with the Spirit. Either the glass is empty or full. Dr. Grudem points out that people are not like that. He says a better analogy would be a balloon because it can be full of air but then it can be more and more full. Like all analogies this one breaks down if you take it too far. The point he makes is that we all need more of the Holy Spirit, and Jesus is the only person who has the Holy Spirit without measure.

As we look at the great evangelists of more recent history we see how many speak of such experiences. John Wesley (1703–1791), the founder of modern Methodism, wrote of an occurrence on New Year's Day 1739:

> At about three in the morning, as we were continuing in prayer, the power of God came mightily upon us. Many cried out in complete joy. Others were knocked to the ground. As soon as we recovered a little from that awe and amazement at God's presence, we broke out in praise.

The result was that "the Holy Spirit began to move among us with amazing power when we met in his name." When anyone fell down under the preaching, they were prayed for until they were "filled with the peace and joy of the Holy Spirit," which was frequently "received in a moment."

Jesus is the only person who has the Holy Spirit without measure.

Wesley's journal is full of such accounts. One Quaker, who objected to such goings-on, "went down as thunderstruck" and rose to cry aloud: "Now I know you are a prophet of the Lord."

Wesley concluded: "Similar experiences continued to increase as I preached. It seemed prudent to preach and write on the work of the Holy Spirit."[10] He preached regularly at Bristol's Newgate prison where the jailer, Abel Dagge, had been converted under Whitefield in 1737.

One Thursday Wesley preached on the text "He that believeth hath everlasting life." At the end he prayed, "If this is thy truth, do not delay to confirm it by signs following." Immediately "the power of God fell among us. One, and another, and another, sank to the earth . . . dropping on all sides as thunderstruck." One, Ann Davies, cried out. He went across and prayed over her and she began to praise God in joy.[11]

For thirty-five years George Whitefield (1714–1770) was the outstanding itinerant preacher in Britain and America and he changed the conventions of preaching, opening the way for mass evangelism. He wrote in his journal: "Was filled with the Holy Ghost. Oh, that all who deny the promise of the Father, might thus receive it themselves! Oh, that all were partakers of my joy!"[12]

Charles Grandison Finney (1792–1875) was one of history's greatest evangelists, considered by many to be the forerunner of modern evangelism. Finney's experience of the Holy Spirit occurred later on the same day as his conversion. He wrote of what happened to him in 1821.

> The Holy Spirit descended upon me in a manner that seemed to go through me, body and soul. I could feel the impression, like a wave of electricity, going through and through me. Indeed, it seemed to come in waves and waves of liquid love; for I could not express it in any other way. And yet it did not seem like water but rather the breath of God. I can recollect distinctly that it seemed to fan me, like immense wings: and it seemed to me, as these waves passed over me, that they literally moved my hair like a passing breeze. No words can express the wonderful love that was shed abroad in my heart. I wept aloud with joy and love; and I do not know but I should say, I literally bellowed out the unutterable gushings of my heart. These waves came over me, and over me, and over me, one after another, until I recollect I cried out, "I shall die if these waves continue to pass over me." I said, "Lord, I cannot bear any more;" yet I had no fear of death.[13]

The same God is at work today among us.

Perhaps the greatest evangelist of the nineteenth century was D. L. Moody (1837–1899). Early in his ministry he was a successful superintendent of a Sunday school mission in Chicago. However, two old ladies in his congregation informed him after a service that they were praying for him because he lacked the power of the Spirit. Although he was annoyed at their suggestion, the more he pondered about it the more he knew they were right. He wrote later that "there came a great hunger into my soul. I did not know what it was. I began to cry out as I never did before. I really felt that I did not want to live if I could not have this power for service. . . . I was crying all the time that God would fill me with His Holy Spirit." [14]

About six months later, as he was walking down Wall Street in New York City, the Holy Spirit came upon him powerfully. He recorded later: "Oh! What a day, I cannot describe it! I seldom refer to it, it is almost too sacred an experience to name. . . . I can only say God revealed Himself to me, and I had such an experience of His love that I had to ask Him to stay His hand."

John Pollock, his biographer, adds that Moody never thirsted again. "The dead, dry days were gone. 'I was all the time tugging and carrying water. But now I have a river that carries me.' "[15]

The next president of the Moody Bible Institute was the great American evangelist of the early twentieth century, R. A. Torrey (1856–1928). In his book *The Baptism with the Holy Spirit* he wrote:

> It was a great turning point in my ministry when, after much thought and study and meditation, I became satisfied that the baptism with the Holy Spirit was an experience for today and for me, and set myself to obtain it. Such blessing came to me personally that I began giving Bible readings on the subject, and I have continued to do so with increasing frequency as the years have passed. . . . It has been the author's unspeakable privilege to pray with many ministers and Christian workers for this great blessing, and after to learn from them or from others of the new power that had come into their service, none other than the power of the Holy Spirit.[16]

In his book *Why God Used D. L. Moody*, Will H. Houghton wrote:

> Some of our readers may take exception to Dr. Torrey's use of the term "the baptism with the Holy Ghost." Perhaps if Dr. Torrey lived in our day and saw some of the wildfire in connection with that expression, he would use some other

phrase. But let no one quibble about an experience as important as the filling of the Spirit. In this little book Dr. Torrey quotes Mr. Moody as saying, in a discussion on this very matter, "Oh, why will they split hairs? Why don't they see that this is just the one thing that they themselves need? They are good teachers, they are wonderful teachers, and I am so glad to have them here, but why will they not see that the baptism of the Holy Ghost is just the one touch that they themselves need?"

I think that there can be little doubt that the greatest evangelist of our century has been Billy Graham (born 1918). In an authorized biography John Pollock tells how Billy Graham visited Hildenborough Hall in 1947 and heard Stephen Olford speak on the subject "Be not drunk—but be filled with the Spirit." Billy Graham asked to see Olford privately and Olford expounded the fullness of the Holy Spirit in the life of a believer. "At the close of the second day they prayed 'like Jacob of old laying hold of God,' " recalls Olford, "crying, 'Lord, I will not let Thee go except Thou bless me,' until we came to a place of rest and praising"; and Graham said, "I'm filled. This is a turning point in my life. This will revolutionize my ministry."[17]

One of the keys to *Alpha* is having a team of Spirit-filled people using every gift they possess to lead others to Christ. Those who come to Christ on the course know that a radical change has occurred in their lives because they have been filled with the Holy Spirit. This experience of God gives them the stimulus and power to invite their friends to the next *Alpha*.

Part II

Setting Up and Running
The Alpha Course

3

Practicalities

Whatever you do, work at it with all your heart, as working for the Lord, not for men, since you know that you will receive an inheritance from the Lord as a reward.
—Colossians 3:23-24

UNDERSTANDING ALPHA

To those attending as guests, *Alpha* is a practical introduction to the Christian faith. To those running the course (The *Alpha* Leader, Director, Small-Group Leaders and Helpers, Worship Team, and Task Force Members), it is friendship-based evangelism.

The following acronym helps explain what *Alpha* is and sums up some of the key ingredients of *Alpha:*

Anyone can come. Anyone interested in finding out more about the Christian faith can be invited on this ten-week introduction designed for nonchurch-goers and new Christians. It can also be used as a refresher course for mature Christians. In many churches the first course is attended mainly by church members and later fringe members and then the unchurched.

Learning and laughter. The course is based on a series of fifteen talks which tackle the key questions at the heart of the Christian faith. (These talks can be given by a leader or there are tapes or videos available depending on group size.) It is possible to learn about the Christian faith and to enjoy the experience! Laughter and fun are a key part of the course, breaking down barriers and enabling everyone to relax together.

Pasta. Eating together gives people the chance to get to know each other and to develop Christian friendships. It is important that the course is held in a welcoming environment.

Helping one another. The small groups encourage everyone to participate and help each other along the way, as they discuss the talks, study the Bible, and pray for each other. For the leaders and helpers, the course provides an opportunity to help bring others to faith. People often come back and help on the next course or bring their friends along to see what it is all about.

Ask anything. *Alpha* is a place where no question is regarded as too simple or too hostile. People are given a chance to raise their questions and discuss relevant topics in small groups after the talk.

Beginning and ending on time . . . is also important.

There are many variables with *Alpha Courses* including the size, location, and time of the course, as well as the number of people needed to run the course. *Alpha Courses* vary in size. Some are very small and some are very large. Courses are held in homes, churches, prisons, and schools. The principles in this chapter apply to all courses regardless of size, location, or time. Since evening courses are most common, this model is explained in detail. If you are planning a daytime *Alpha*, read about evening *Alpha* and then go to page 64 where daytime *Alpha* is explained in depth. The expected attendance determines the number of people needed to run the course. Suggested organizational charts begin on page 54 and job descriptions begin on page 115.

EVENING ALPHA

Alpha is often held at night when most people are available to attend. There are several important parts of evening *Alpha*—a simple dinner, a talk on some aspect of the Christian faith, informal interaction within preassigned small groups, a weekend retreat, and a celebration dinner which serves as the end of one course and the beginning of the next.

A typical evening

While the actual schedule may vary depending on location and day of the week, a typical evening will look something like this:

5:15 or 5:30 P.M.	Leaders and helpers meet to pray
6:00 P.M.	Dinner is served
6:30 P.M.	Welcome
6:40 P.M.	Songs of worship
6:50 P.M.	Talk
7:45 P.M.	Coffee
8:00 P.M.	Small groups
9:00 P.M.	End

The meeting of the leaders and helpers at the beginning of the evening for prayer and organization is of great importance. Beginning and ending on time each week is also important.

Dinner. Serve dinner at 6:00 P.M. Dinner is an important aspect of *Alpha.* People often feel more relaxed when visiting over a meal. Avoid "religious" conversation during dinner. The leaders and helpers should keep the conversation on personal, everyday things. This is a time to get to know the guests as individuals.

Often people have commented that the food kept them coming back to *Alpha,* so it is worth keeping the food at a high standard!

When *Alpha* is small (around twelve people), each person, starting with the leaders and helpers, can take turns cooking dinner. As it grows and there are up to about ten small groups, each small group can take a turn to cook. (Make sure you have enough paper plates and cups, coffee cups, knives, forks, spoons, tea, coffee, milk, and other beverages, etc.) If you don't have a Task Force, the group who cooked should do the cleaning up and dishes.

Some suggestions for *Alpha* meals would include simple pasta dishes, sloppy joes, chili con carne, and pizza. Make sure you have a vegetarian alternative. Serve the main dish with a salad or gelatin, bread or rolls, and a simple dessert.

While there is no registration fee for the *Alpha Course,* request a small contribution for the meal each evening and for the food and lodging during the weekend. If a group is doing the cooking, the cost can usually be kept to approximately $2.50 to $3.00 per person. Place baskets for contributions at the serving points and reimburse whoever paid for the food. If you have a caterer, make the actual cost known and ask people to pay whatever they feel they can afford.

Eating together is an essential part of the course, as it gives people the chance to get to know others in a relaxed way. Friendships grow throughout the course, especially within the small groups, in an extraordinary way.

> Dinner . . . is a time to get to know the guests as individuals.

Welcome and worship. At 6:30 P.M. welcome everyone and promote books and tapes related to that evening's talk. (Suggested titles are listed on pages 151-152 in this book and at the end of each session in *The Alpha Course Manual* and *Leader's Guide*). To help everyone relax, tell some kind of joke.

Humor is an important part of the course and these jokes are usually appreciated out of all proportion to their merit! It is important for outsiders to see that Christians have a sense of humor and that laughter and faith in Jesus Christ are not incompatible. Beginning around Week 3 or 4 use this time to promote the weekend, and from Week 6 begin talking about the Celebration Dinner at the end of the course.

At 6:40 P.M. have a short period of singing. Make sure to explain carefully what you are going to do. I often quote what the apostle Paul says in his letter to the Ephesians, "Speak to one another with psalms, hymns

We . . . change gradually from singing about God to singing directly to Him.

and spiritual songs. Sing and make music in your heart to the Lord" (Eph. 5:19). I explain that we are going to sing a mixture of psalms (usually set to modern melodies), hymns, and spiritual songs. We have a mixture of old and new. We always start the first night with a well-known hymn for the benefit of those who might find that more familiar. As the course goes on we tend toward more modern songs, changing gradually from singing about God to singing directly to Him. We also increase the length of time we spend in worship from about five minutes on the first night to about fifteen to twenty minutes toward the end of the course. We try not to move too quickly at the beginning, and I explain that what matters is that we "sing and make music in our hearts." Some may not be ready to participate and it is fine for them simply to listen until they are ready to join in.

The Worship Leader must sound confident, even if he or she is not. It is better that the Worship Leader give no introduction to the songs. This person is there to lead worship rather than to give what easily becomes another talk. Unless worship can be led and music played competently it is probably better not done at all. Some *Alpha Courses* run without any singing. The very small courses who listen to the tapes or watch the video would not normally have any singing.

Although many find the singing the most difficult part of the course to begin with, and some are even hostile toward it, by the end they often find it is the part they value most. For many, such singing is their first experience of communicating with God. It also helps people to make the step from *Alpha* to the church where the worship of God is central.

The talk. After the singing comes the talk. This may be given by the *Alpha* Leader or presented on videotape or audiotape (The *Alpha Course Videos* come in a set of five videotapes with three talks on each tape; The *Alpha Course* Tapes include fifteen audiocassettes, each with one talk). Because there are so many details to setting up an *Alpha Course* for the first time, many churches find it easiest to start with the talks on video and gradually shift to live speakers. In the long run this is probably best. On smaller courses it is probably better to have a variety of speakers. On larger ones it is necessary to have someone who is used to speaking to more sizable gatherings. This inevitably limits the number of speakers available. Chapter 5 offers some insights on preparing and giving effective talks.

The talk for Week 1 is "Who Is Jesus?" (chapter 2 in *Questions of Life* and *The Alpha Course Manual;* page 21 in *The Alpha Course Leader's Guide*). During Weeks 2–6 cover the material in chapters 3–7 of *Questions of Life.* The weekend away works best following Week 6; however, this may vary due to each individual situation.

Following is a suggested sequence of fifteen *Alpha* talks. The number in parentheses after each title is the corresponding chapter in *Questions of Life* and *The Alpha Course Manual* and the corresponding talk on the *Alpha Course* videotapes or audiotapes. It is best to have the talk on God's guidance (#7) before the weekend away and before the talk titled "How Can I Resist Evil?" (#7). The talk about avoiding evil needs to always come after the weekend away. This is because the talk about spiritual warfare only becomes truly relevant after people have experienced the power of the Holy Spirit.

WEEK	TITLE
1	Who Is Jesus? (#2)
2	Why Did Jesus Die? (#3)
3	How Can I Be Sure of My Faith? (#4)
4	Why and How Should I Read the Bible? (#5)
5	Why and How Do I Pray? (#6)
6	How Does God Guide Us? (#7)
WEEKEND RETREAT	
	Who Is the Holy Spirit? (#8)
	What Does the Holy Spirit Do? (#9)
	How Can I Be Filled with the Spirit? (#10)
	How Can I Make the Most of the Rest of My Life? (#15)
7	How Can I Resist Evil? (#11)
8	Why and How Should We Tell Others? (#12)
9	Does God Heal Today? (#13)
10	What About the Church? (#14)
11	Celebration (or *Alpha*) Dinner "Christianity: Boring, Untrue, and Irrelevant?" (#1)

The talk for Week 8 is "Why and How Should We Tell Others?" This is an excellent time to promote the *Alpha* dinner party or Celebration Dinner which is held at the end of the course (see page 52 in this chapter). Following the talk on healing (Week 9) there are no small groups due to a time of ministry (see chapter 7 in this book).

For Week 10 the subject is the church. The main aim of this talk is to start integrating those who have been attending *Alpha* into the life of the church. If your church has ongoing small groups or home groups, encourage *Alpha* guests to join such a group. Often a whole small group from *Alpha* will join the same home group or small group.

Each group should not exceed 12 people.

Small groups. At the end of the talk for Weeks 1–8 and 10, everyone meets in small groups (see chapter 5 in this book). Each group should not exceed 12 people with two leaders and two helpers. It is important to end the groups promptly at 9:00 P.M. or the designated time. People need to know when they can count on heading for home.

During the final small-group time, distribute a copy of the *"Alpha Questionnaire"* (see Appendix E, page 145) to each person and allow time to complete the questions before everyone leaves. Use the responses to these surveys to help you see how the course needs to be improved next time.

If you have people who are interested in *Alpha* but cannot attend during the evening, consider a daytime *Alpha* Course. Details are included beginning on page 64.

Resources and related reading. The *Alpha* Leader needs to be very familiar with the content of this book, especially chapters 4, 5, and 6 which are used in training the Ministry Team. If the course leader is also giving the talks, he or she needs to master the content of *Questions of Life.*

The Director will use the information in this book to set up and run the course. Permission is granted to photocopy all of the appendices, but not the chapters.

Each leader and helper (the Ministry Team) needs a copy of *Questions of Life, The Alpha Course Manual,* and *The Alpha Course Leader's Guide.* It is also helpful for each leader and even helpers to have access to a copy of this book and *Searching Issues* (contains answers to the seven most-asked questions during *Alpha*). Guests receive a copy of *Why Jesus?*[2] at the *Alpha* Dinner (or *Why Christmas?*[3] if it is Christmastime) and a copy of *The Alpha Course Manual* during Week 1. There is a list of related, recommended books at the end of each session in *The Manual* and *Leader's Guide* (and on pages 151-152 in this book). Ideally, a book table should be open for the whole evening (except during the talk) so that people may purchase any books they prefer. If the *Alpha* talk is given live by the *Alpha* Leader, ensure that the previous weeks' talks are available on tape so that anyone who misses a session can buy the tape. If you use the *Alpha Course Videos* or *Tapes,* have sets of the audiotapes available for loan to those who may want to review or catch a missed talk.

The first night

Greeters. Your Greeters (who are usually Small-Group Helpers) are going to be the first people your guests see. Often people arrive with many preconceived ideas of what Christians are like, so when they are greeted by a "normal" person they are often surprised and it is very important that their first impression is a good one.

The Greeters need an alphabetical list of guests with the name of their group leaders and the group number. They need to know how many men and how many women are in each group. This is helpful when unexpected guests arrive and need to be placed very quickly in a group. Greeters should also know the names of the group leaders and helpers and the location of each group.

Name tags. Every person should have a name tag with the appropriate group number on it. Make sure that the names are spelled correctly—accuracy is very important. Display the name tags in alphabetical order and delegate one or two people to hand them out (these people might be Runners or Greeters). Give *Alpha* Team Members a different colored name tag so that guests can identify them as leaders and ask them any questions. Keep some spare name tags and a list of unexpected guests who come. Use this list to make a printed name tag for each "surprise" guest for the following week. It is helpful to use the name tags through Week 3 at least.

Runners. If your course is large enough to have several small groups, you will need some of the Small-Group Helpers to also serve as Runners. Runners will meet the guests at the door and take them to their groups. This is especially important for the first three weeks or until everyone is familiar with the routine. Don't ask Small-Group Leaders to be Runners also as they will need to be in their groups to meet people. Again, remember that first impressions are important. The Runners must be careful to remember the name, group number, and location of each group. A Greeter should introduce the guest to a Runner who will get the guest a name tag and take him or her to the correct small group and make introductions to the group leader. The Runner returns quickly to the main door. Obviously, Greeters and Runners should be friendly, but not effusive, as this can overwhelm guests on the first night.

Address lists. Give each small group a blank form for them to fill in names, addresses, and telephone numbers. Stress to all the guests that this is not so that they will be sent junk mail or phoned when they don't come back to the course. Rather the lists are available so that rides may be arranged

Protect the privacy of your guests.

and guests may be contacted if there is any problem such as cancellation due to weather. These lists are then typed up and one copy is returned to the Group Leader each week until Week 4. Do not give each member of the group a copy of the list. If they want to exchange addresses and telephone numbers they can do so within the group. Protect the privacy of your guests. If a guest calls the church office for a telephone number of another guest, do not give details under any circumstances.

At the end of the first evening of the course all the leaders and helpers should meet together briefly to discuss and review the evening.

The weekend

The weekend retreat or weekend away is an essential part of the course. This time is devoted to teaching on the work of the Holy Spirit in the individual lives of those on the course. The material covered during the weekend is in chapters 8, 9, 10, and 15 of *Questions of Life* and Talks 8, 9, 10, and 15 on *The Alpha Course Videos* or *Tapes*. Also included on Video 3 is a short introduction to the weekend. If an entire weekend away is not feasible, it is possible to cover this material in a single day. Sometimes churches hold an all-day local retreat on a Saturday. However, there are tremendous advantages to the weekend away.

Friendships are formed over an entire weekend much more easily than on a single day. As people travel together, have meals together, go for walks, enjoy the Saturday night entertainment, and receive Communion together on Sunday morning, there is a cementing of friendships which have begun to form in the early weeks. It is in this relaxed environment that people unwind and some of the barriers begin to come down. Many make as much progress spiritually during the weekend away as in all the rest of the course put together.

Sometimes it is hard to find an affordable location, but it is usually possible if plans are made far enough ahead. If members of the congregation cannot afford the expense of an entire weekend at a retreat center or hotel, then the weekend could take place in a local setting. However, in most congregations those who can afford to pay are willing to help those who cannot by contributing all or a portion of the cost.

Following are two schedules for the weekend: one for an entire weekend and one for a Saturday only.

Full weekend schedule

Friday

5:30 P.M. onward	Arrive
7:00 P.M.	Dinner
9:15 P.M.	Worship and a brief introduction to the weekend. This can include a short talk based on John 15 or perhaps a testimony.

Saturday

8:00 A.M.	Breakfast
9:00 A.M.	Worship
	Talk 1 - "Who Is the Holy Spirit?" (on Video 3, #8)
10:15 A.M.	Coffee
10:45 A.M.	Talk 2 - "What Does the Holy Spirit Do?" (on Video 3, #9)
11:30 A.M.	Small group discussion. Often we look at 1 Corinthians 12:1-11 and the subject of spiritual gifts. This gives people a chance to discuss and air their fears.
12:30 P.M.	Lunch
Free Afternoon	Activities can be organized e.g., sports, walks, etc.
3:30 P.M.	Optional refreshments
4:00 P.M.	Worship
	Talk 3 - "How Can I Be Filled with the Spirit?" (on Video 4, #10)
6:00 P.M.	Dinner
8:00 P.M.	Talent Show (A variety of skits and songs without anything distasteful, religious, or nasty. Participation is voluntary!)

Sunday

9:00 A.M.	Breakfast
9:45 A.M.	Small group discussion. Often we talk about how each member of the group is doing.
10:30 A.M.	Worship
	Talk 4 - "How Can I Make the Most of the Rest of My Life?" (on Video 5, #15)
	Communion
1:00 P.M.	Lunch
Free Afternoon	Hopefully everybody meets again at the evening service at church!

The *Alpha* Dinner is the wrap-up for one course and the kickoff of the next course.

All-day Saturday only	
8:00 A.M.	Arrive
8:30 A.M.	Worship
	Talk 1 - Combine "Who Is the Holy Spirit?" and "What Does the Holy Spirit Do?" (on Video 3, #8 and #9)
9:45 A.M.	Coffee
10:15 A.M.	Talk 2 - "How Can I Be Filled with the Spirit? (on Video 4, #10)
Noon	Lunch
1:15 P.M.	Free Afternoon
3:00 P.M.	Optional refreshments
4:00 P.M.	Worship
	Talk 3 - "How Can I Make the Most of the Rest of My Life?" (on Video 5, #15)
6:30 P.M.	Depart

More details about the weekend are included in the job descriptions for the Weekend Retreat Coordinator (see page 126) and the Weekend Entertainment Coordinator (see page 128).

The Celebration Dinner

The *Alpha* Dinner serves two purposes: it is the wrap-up for one course and the kickoff of the next course.

For your first *Alpha Course,* hold a dinner party before the course starts, then hold one at the end of every course so that guests on the course can invite their friends. You will begin to promote the dinner around Week 7 and at the same time start collecting money for the party. Everyone should pay for their guests as well as for themselves.

On Week 8 (when the talk is on "Why and How Should We Tell Others?"), advertise the dinner and give out the invitations. This will enable you to confirm the number of people coming by Week 10. When *Alpha* at Holy Trinity Brompton was small, each person would bring a certain amount of food. These days we use caterers, since we now have over a thousand people attending, and those on the course contribute as they are able, bearing in mind the number of guests they intend to bring. If the number of people attending the Celebration Dinner exceeds a comfortable room capacity, consider holding two smaller dinners. We have been doing this at Holy Trinity Brompton for some time with great success. We have a dinner on each of the two Wednesdays following Week 10.

The Celebration Dinner begins at 6:00 P.M. when everyone gathers for beverages followed by a sit-down dinner together. To avoid embarrassing guests or making guests uncomfortable, we do not say grace.

All the details for the Celebration Dinner will be handled by a coordinator and team preferably made up of those who are not inviting friends. It is important to do everything possible to create a good atmosphere. Make a seating plan and set the tables with tablecloths, nice dinnerware, flowers, and candles. The talk should come after eating and during coffee. See the job description for the *Alpha* Dinner Coordinator on page 121 for more details about the Celebration Dinner.

It is important to do everything possible to create a good atmosphere.

After a leisurely dinner, I welcome everyone. We usually thank those people who have organized the evening. I then invite one or two people who have attended the course to speak about what has happened in their lives, giving them a minimum of advance notice so that they do not have too long to worry about it. I do not allow them any notes as it always comes out best when they speak from their hearts about their own experience, and I always interview them so that they do not need to worry about forgetting what to say.

After the interview I give a talk along the lines of "Christianity: Boring, Untrue, and Irrelevant?" (chapter 1 in *Questions of Life;* Talk 1 in the *Alpha Course* Videos or *Alpha Course* Tapes). If the party is at Christmas, I give a similar talk but based around the theme "What Is the Point of Christmas?"

At the end of the talk I usually refer to Paul's experience in Athens where he found there was one of three reactions to what he had said about Jesus (see Acts 17: 32-34).

• "Some of them sneered." I point out that that was my own position for many years, so I am not judging them if they take the same position.

• Others said, "We want to hear you again on this subject" (vs. 32). I suggest that those who feel like that come to the next *Alpha Course* for which we have invitations and brochures are available.

• "A few . . . believed" (vs. 34). For the benefit of these, I ask everyone to bow their heads for a prayer and then I pray a prayer aloud along the lines of the one in the back of the booklet *Why Jesus?* There are usually some, I discover afterward, who pray the prayer that night.

I then encourage anyone interested to come to the first evening of the next *Alpha Course* at least. I offer every guest a copy of *Why Jesus?* or *Why Christmas?* as appropriate, and invite them to stay for coffee, dessert, and informal talking. Most of them stay and talk with the friends they came with and then the evening ends.

Many of those who come to the supper wish to do an *Alpha Course* as soon as possible. Hence it is vital that there is one planned immediately thereafter.

Aim to get everything 100 percent right.

The *Alpha* Dinner is one of the reasons why so many people come on each *Alpha Course*. We have found that each *Alpha* supper has been bigger than the one before and each *Alpha Course* likewise has been bigger than the one before. Therefore, it is good to make sure that people are organized to set tables, serve, and clean up, or chaos may ensue.

SETTING UP AND RUNNING THE ALPHA COURSE

There is a lot of hard work behind the scenes of an *Alpha Course* and every job is vitally important. Aim to get everything 100 percent right. Guests who come on the course will see that every effort has been made and that everything is run in an efficient way.

PREPARATION

It is essential to begin planning for your *Alpha Course* six to nine months in advance. This allows you to select and train an *Alpha* Team and to promote the course effectively. A detailed timeline begins on page 129.

Some of the following information will apply only to larger courses, where the first thing the *Alpha* Leader should do is to appoint the Director (or Administrator). The number of people needed to run an *Alpha Course* will vary depending on the number of expected guests.

Study the following sample organizational charts and adapt one to fit the number of guests or small groups you anticipate. Reproducible job descriptions for all positions begin on page 113.

Small Alpha Courses

For a course of less than twenty-five people (or 1 or 2 small groups), the *Alpha* Leader and the Director usually run the entire program. The *Alpha* Leader either gives the talks or introduces the recorded talk each week and provides spiritual leadership, while the Director oversees the practical aspects such as the meal and weekend away. Both the *Alpha* Leader and the Director will lead or help lead a small group. Each person (including the guests) will take a turn preparing dinner. The organizational chart for this size ministry looks something like this:

> **Organizational Chart**
> Small *Alpha Courses* (1 or 2 small groups; under 25 people)
> *Alpha* Leader
> |
> *Alpha* Director
> |
> Small-Group Helpers

Medium Alpha Courses

If you expect between 25 and 120 people (or 3 to 9 groups), adapt the following organizational chart to meet your needs. Note that the Director will serve as the Small-Group Coordinator, while Task Force Members will help greet, work at the book table (if you have one), serve, and cleanup each week. The Ministry Team will be primarily the Small-Group Leaders and Helpers, along with the *Alpha* Leader and Director.

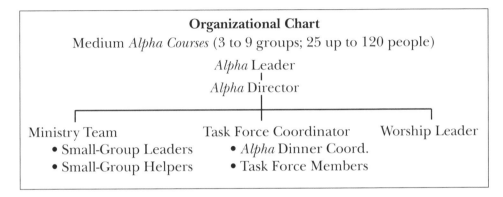

Organizational Chart
Medium *Alpha Courses* (3 to 9 groups; 25 up to 120 people)

Alpha Leader

Alpha Director

Ministry Team
• Small-Group Leaders
• Small-Group Helpers

Task Force Coordinator
• *Alpha* Dinner Coord.
• Task Force Members

Worship Leader

Large Alpha Courses

Once a course reaches 120 people (or ten small groups) or more, the work load increases significantly. Therefore more workers are needed. Adapt the following organizational chart to meet your needs.

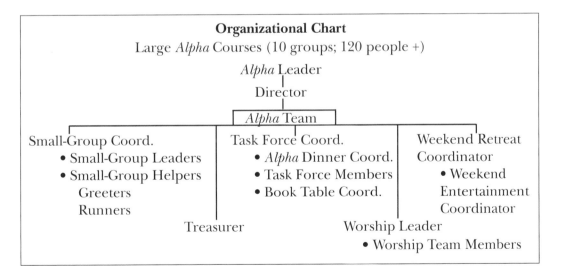

Organizational Chart
Large *Alpha* Courses (10 groups; 120 people +)

Alpha Leader

Director

Alpha Team

Small-Group Coord.
• Small-Group Leaders
• Small-Group Helpers
Greeters
Runners

Task Force Coord.
• *Alpha* Dinner Coord.
• Task Force Members
• Book Table Coord.

Weekend Retreat
Coordinator
• Weekend
Entertainment
Coordinator

Treasurer

Worship Leader
• Worship Team Members

TEAM SELECTION

One of the most important aspects of an *Alpha Course* is a leadership team. It is vital to get the right people. Courses of all sizes need Small-Group

Many helpers are those who have just finished the previous course.

Leaders and Helpers. First, contact the small-group or home-group leaders of the church and ask them to suggest people who would be good *Alpha* Small-Group Leaders and Helpers. It is important to emphasize commitment to the course, because if the leaders are not consistent in coming, then there is no reason why anybody else should come either.

Small-Group Leaders

Approximately one-third of the course members should be leaders or helpers. Each small group is made up of around 12 people including three or four leaders and helpers who need to be selected very carefully. The leaders must be those who appear to have the beginnings of a gift of evangelism and are sensitive, encouraging, and easy to get along with. They do not necessarily need to be longtime Christians, but one indication of this gift of evangelism is that they are "good with people."

This is the test I often use when someone suggests another person—say John—as a leader: "Suppose you had a nonchurchgoing friend for whom you had been praying for several years; would you be totally confident about putting that person in John's group?" If the answer is "No" or "He'd be great with other people," the person is probably not suitable to be a leader of a small group on *Alpha*. If the answer is "Yes," then the person is likely to be a good leader.

Small-Group Helpers

Each small group also has one or two helpers, usually one man and one woman. They might be a couple or two single people. Try not to have a dating couple lead or help with the same group, as complications can arise if the relationship breaks up halfway through the course. The ideal is to have one couple and two single people on the leadership team of each small group.

The helpers should pass the same test as the leaders but they may be relatively new Christians. Occasionally they may not even be Christians at all. Many helpers are those who have just finished the previous course. Some ask to come back and do the course again. In many cases I would ask them to come back as helpers. I strongly discourage anyone from simply repeating the course. I do not want people to get stuck doing *Alpha* over and over again as they need to move on in their journey of faith. One of the ways of moving on is to come back and help others. People who have recently done the course are often specially sensitive to the fears and doubts of members of their group. They can empathize with them, saying, "I felt that way too," or "I found that difficult." This removes the "we" and "they" barrier.

It is vital that all the team . . . are trained.

Ask the leaders of the previous course to recommend small-group members who would be good at helping. Watch for those who would make good helpers and ask them to come back and help. Many of them are new Christians and many have lots of friends who are not Christians. Quite a high percentage of the next course will be friends of those who are helping. This is one of the ways in which the course grows.

Task Force

If the course is large it is helpful to have a Task Force to perform practical tasks such as greeting, setting up, serving, and cleaning up. This group is vital to the smooth running of the course. In this way very few people from the course will be asked to help with the more mundane tasks and will therefore not be distracted from their enjoyment of *Alpha*. The Task Force should be welcome to listen to the talks and should be given as much encouragement as possible. Always cherish your Task Force!

At Holy Trinity Brompton we have a remarkable group on the Task Force. They are people who either do not want to be in a small group or would not be suitable as Small-Group Leaders or Helpers but have "the gift of helps" (from 1 Cor. 12:28). They are like the group chosen in the Book of Acts to "wait on tables" (Acts 6: 2). They are men and women who are full of the Spirit and willing to serve in any capacity. Their love and service alone are a powerful witness of the love of Christ to those who are on the course. A key appointment is the Task Force Coordinator who assigns tasks and offers pastoral care. A full job description for this person is on page 120 in Appendix A.

TEAM TRAINING

It is vital that all the team (including those who have been Christians for many years) are trained. Insist that all leaders and helpers come to the training sessions. If they are unable to come, ask them to listen to the tape or view the video. Even if some of your team have helped on several *Alpha Courses,* they should come to every training session of every course. Even if one of your leaders has been leading small groups for twenty years or so, stress that *Alpha* small groups are very different.

Small-Group Leaders and Helpers and Task Force Members attend three training sessions as follows:

Two weeks prior to course	Session 1	Leading Small Groups
One week prior to course	Session 2	Pastoral Care
Week prior to weekend away	Session 3	Ministry during *Alpha*

Content of these three training sessions is contained in chapters 5, 6, and 7 of this book, Part I of *The Alpha Course Leader's Guide*, and the entirety of the *Alpha Leaders Training Video* or *Alpha Leaders Training Tapes*. (See page 154 for ordering information.) Training sessions are run similar to evening *Alpha*:

6:00 P.M.	Dinner
6:45 P.M.	Worship and prayer
7:00 P.M.	Training talk
8:00 P.M.	Discussion of talk
9:00 P.M.	End of training

It is recommended that all leaders and helpers read three books before the course begins: *Questions of Life, Searching Issues*, and this book (*How to Run the Alpha Course* which is based on *Telling Others*). It is important that the team members spend time together and get to know each other before the course begins. Do not assume that they already know each other very well. After the training talk give an opportunity to ask questions either relating to the talk or about any other aspect of the *Alpha Course*. At this point cover some of the administrative details and prepare people for the jobs they will be asked to do on the first evening and thereafter. Job descriptions for all positions are included in Appendix A beginning on page 111.

Throughout the training and the course, stress the importance of praying for every aspect of *Alpha*. Ask the leaders and helpers to commit themselves to pray for every member of their group regularly.

Small-Group assignments

This can be a very long task, so allow plenty of time. Be firm with your team, emphasizing that everyone should be willing to do anything from leading to cleanup.

Arrange groups primarily by age and think carefully about the dynamics of the group: the balance of personalities, social backgrounds, professions, etc. If your church has home groups or other small groups, it is also good to select a team from the same group so that there can be continuity for the guests after the course. Regardless, it is best to put together a team who will work well with one another. Allocate a specific

It is best to put together a team who will work well with one another.

person in each group to look after the administration for their group, preferably someone who is gifted in that area and who can definitely come to the administration/prayer meetings prior to *Alpha* every week.

Often you will have very little information about your guests. From the registration form you may only have their name, address, telephone number, an idea of their age, and their handwriting!

Remember that these are individuals. At Holy Trinity we pray over almost every single registration and ask for guidance. If people are not happy in their groups, they might not come back, so it is very important to get it right. If there is a genuine reason why someone should move to a different group (such as a large age gap with the rest of the group), do it in the first week. Otherwise it is disruptive for those in the old group as well as the new one.

If a guest is a friend of someone on the team, try to find out as much as possible about the guest which will help you to put them in the right group. Quite often it is better not to put the guest in the same group as their friend who is helping as he or she often feels inhibited and unable to ask questions. Always put married couples in the same group unless specifically asked to do otherwise.

Aim to finalize this task on the last day before the course starts. In this way last-minute applications will be on your list, assigned a group, and have a preprinted name tag.

Emphasize to all leaders, helpers, and Task Force Members that their commitment is not just for eleven weeks (including the Celebration Dinner) but also for three training nights. Leaders and helpers will also need to commit to social evenings with their group, follow-up after the course has finished, getting group members into an ongoing small group or home group, and integrating them into the church.

THE ALPHA CONFERENCE

Many churches have found it helpful to attend an *Alpha* Conference before running their own *Alpha Course*. *Alpha* Conferences are held throughout North America and in many other countries around the world. The purpose of an *Alpha* Conference is to expose interested church staff and laypersons to the ministry of *Alpha* and to help them understand the principles and practicalities of setting up and running an *Alpha Course*. For information about upcoming conferences, in the United States call 1-800-36-ALPHA (1-800-362-5742), or in Canada call 1-800-263-2664.

The content of the chapters and Appendices C, E, and F of this book are an *Alpha* Conference in written form. The entire conference is available on audiotape (*Alpha Conference Talks on Tape*) and the first two

Decide who will be invited to attend the first course.

sessions are available on videotape (*How to Run the Alpha Course Video*). For ordering information see page 154.

THE FIRST COURSE

It is vitally important to decide who will be invited to attend the first course. Is your purpose to reach those on the fringe of the church from the first course on? Or is it initially to expose the church members to the *Alpha* ministry and then reach out beyond your active membership?

If you answer yes to the first question, the way to start is simply to begin with a small group of anyone interested and allow it to grow from there. If you want everyone in the church to experience *Alpha*, you will start with a large course introducing *Alpha* to the whole church.

Either option is valid as long as your expectations meet the likely results. Experience has shown that with option one, the numbers start small and gradually build. With the second option, the numbers begin large, drop off for a time, and then rebuild gradually.

There are two advantages to starting with a large course:

- Everyone in the church can see what *Alpha* is and how it works. Hopefully this will build confidence in the course and those attending will invite friends or relatives to the second course.
- *Alpha* may act as a renewal program in the church.

There are also two possible disadvantages with this method:

- Those people from the fringe of the church and beyond are less likely to feel at home during a course which is predominately church members.
- There could be an anticlimactic feel as the second course may be smaller than the first.

Among churches who run the first course for the entire church there tends to be a sharp drop in numbers for the second course. This is because everyone in the church has already attended and then they need to reach out beyond the church core. For example, the first course might have 50 to 100 people attend.

Because many or even most church members have attended, the second course may drop to only 10 or 15 people. It is important that the church is not discouraged by the decreased attendance. It is likely that the smaller group will include fringe members or even outsiders. Thus *Alpha* will begin to fulfill its true function—that is, to draw those outside the church.

If even one or two guests come to Christ they will become excited about Jesus and bring along their family and friends to the next course. As the momentum builds, each subsequent course will be slightly bigger. The numbers might look something like this:

Remember that ideally *Alpha* is an ongoing ministry of evangelism.

First Course	50–100
Second Course	10–15+
Third Course	15–20+
Fourth Course	25–50, etc.

It is important to remember that ideally *Alpha* is an ongoing ministry of evangelism. It may take a few courses to work out the details of getting started and for church members to gain the confidence to invite their friends or associates. At the beginning stages it is important to persevere and not be discouraged if the numbers drop. In time, the effect of new Christians reaching their friends has a ripple effect and the numbers begin to grow.

Dates

The next step to an effective *Alpha Course* is to set the dates. Make sure that your *Alpha Course* does not conflict with anything that will keep people from coming, such as Thanksgiving, the Christmas holidays, Easter, or summer vacations. Remember to allow enough time for the two training sessions before the course begins and the Celebration Dinner at the end of the course. The best times are:

- Fall session (late September or early October through early December),
- Winter session (January through March or between Christmas and Easter), and
- Spring session (April through early June or after Easter).

It is best for the fall session to finish a week or two before Christmas, the winter session to begin a week or two after Christmas and finish before Easter, and the spring session to end before schools are out for the summer.

The course takes eleven weeks (including the *Alpha* Dinner at the beginning of your first *Alpha Course* or the Celebration Dinner party at the end of each subsequent course). *Alpha* at Holy Trinity Brompton takes place on Wednesday evenings. Another option is a daytime *Alpha* as described on pages 64-68 in this book. If you are doing daytime *Alpha*, tie in the course with the school calendar. It is of utmost importance, in order to maintain the momentum, to run at least three courses a year. When people complete *Alpha* they very often want to invite their families and friends to the next course.

Location

> **!** Whatever the setting, it should be "unchurchy."

To start, the ideal venue is a home because such an environment is unthreatening for those who do not go to church. For many years the *Alpha Course* at Holy Trinity Brompton was run in a home, and we had considerable hesitations about moving to a different setting. We only did so eventually because of the increasing size of the course. When the course outgrows the home, a new location needs to be found with a welcoming atmosphere. If the course is held in a church, it is best to meet in a room other than the sanctuary or worship center. Those who are unchurched are most comfortable in a neutral setting.

Whatever the setting, it should be "unchurchy." It can often be difficult to make a church hall look welcoming. If you must use the church remember these tips:

- Use standard lamps instead of overhead fluorescent lighting.
- Provide flowers.
- Cover unattractive tables.
- Adjust temperature.
- Arrange the chairs so that guests can eat together in their groups.
- Make sure that there is good lighting on the speaker and that everyone is able to hear. This may involve arranging a PA system.
- Provide space to hang coats and a secure place for briefcases, purses, and other bags.
- Display signs for directions to rest rooms, book sales, and small-group locations.

Promotion

Promotion of the *Alpha Course* is important so that those outside the church and those on its fringes can be attracted. This can be done through brochures, during worship services on special "*Alpha* Sundays," and at the Celebration Dinner at the end of the course. Once the congregation has confidence in the course they will invite their friends.

Brochure. A quality registration brochure accompanied by a letter is an effective method of promotion. Either prepare an attractive brochure with all the relevant details or purchase packets of fifty full-color brochures with instructions for customizing them for your *Alpha Course* from the publisher (see page 154 for ordering information). If you create your own brochure, permission is granted to reproduce the *Alpha* logo. Alternatively, produce a simple letter which sets out all the dates with a tear-off slip at the bottom.

 The best people to interview are those who do not volunteer.

Fringe. Many people within a church have friends who attend only occasionally, perhaps only on holidays. These people on the fringe are prime candidates to attend *Alpha.* As an Anglican church, we also encourage adults who are preparing for baptism, parents wanting to have their children baptized, and confirmation candidates to do the course. I even encourage couples who are intending to get married in the church to attend *Alpha* as part of their marriage preparation. Some have said to me that it was the best possible marriage preparation as it transformed not only their relationship with God but also their relationship with each other. We would also advertise the course at services which attract those on the fringe, such as the services at Christmas and Easter.

Guest Services/Alpha Sundays. Designate the two Sundays prior to the beginning of the *Alpha Course* as "*Alpha* Sundays." At Holy Trinity Brompton the first Sunday is a regular service with a testimony advertising *Alpha.* I explain what *Alpha* is (using the mnemonic at the start of this chapter). Then I interview someone who has just done the course. I choose someone with whom people will find it easy to identify and about whom they cannot say, "I can see why he or she needs Christianity, but it's not for me."

The best people to interview are those who do not volunteer. This is because if they agree, then they are only speaking for the benefit of others and not for themselves. Ask people about ten minutes beforehand. If they are asked any further in advance they begin to write things down and the interview loses its freshness and power. In those ten minutes ask them the same questions you will really ask them later. This gives you a chance to pick up on anything interesting and it allows them a chance to practice. I also give them lots of reassurance that all will be well! In an interview I normally ask them to say something about what they felt about Christianity before the course, what happened to them, and the changes it has made in their lives. I ask them to avoid glittering generalizations. Rather they should be specific and give concrete examples of the changes that have occurred.

The second Sunday is a guest service which is designed especially for church members to invite their friends and family. This service is low-key and the sermon is evangelistic and challenging. Again *Alpha* would be

The most effective way of advertising . . . is the . . . Celebration Dinner.

advertised and a testimony heard. *Alpha* brochures and complimentary copies of *Why Jesus?* are given to everyone at the end.

These services are designed to make it easy for people to bring their friends who would not normally go to church. Keep the service short and specifically aim the talk at the questions often raised by non-Christians such as "What is the meaning of life?" or "Isn't Christianity a crutch?" At the end of the talk suggest that those who would like to investigate Christianity further come along to *Alpha.* Be careful not to ask them to identify themselves as most of those who are not used to going to church wish to remain anonymous.

I suggest they come along to the first night of *Alpha.* I tell them that if they don't want to come back after that first night, no one is going to call them or send them junk mail. This takes the pressure off them. Most who come to the first night continue to come of their own accord.

Celebration Dinner. The most effective way of advertising an *Alpha Course* is through the Celebration Dinner at the end of the course. This provides an opportunity for guests to invite their friends and families to see what they have been doing for the last ten weeks. It is helpful to encourage people to think about who they will invite to the closing dinner as early as Week 6 or 7. See page 52 for more details about the Celebration Dinner.

DAYTIME ALPHA[4]

Daytime *Alpha* is held on a weekday morning and was originally designed for those who found it easier to attend a course during the day. There are several groups of people who attend including mothers of young children, those who are self-employed or unemployed, and those who prefer not to venture out alone at night. At Holy Trinity Brompton this has generally been a group for women, but recently each group included one or two men.

The daytime *Alpha Course* has proved as successful as the evening course as a means of evangelism. This course, with its appeal to both the head and the heart, has seen many people come into relationship with Christ—from those very far away from Christianity to those who have sat in pews in churches for much of their lives but have not understood that the heart of the Christian faith is a relationship with Jesus. One team member, who had brought about twelve people from her own church to do the morning course at Holy Trinity Brompton, said at the end of the ten weeks that she had sat for years in the church with these people and none of them had moved in any real way toward conversion. Now, many had been converted during the course and they all wanted to attend another *Alpha Course.*

As with evening *Alpha*, we use an simple acronym to help people understand *Alpha*. This one is just slightly different.

Anyone can come.
Laughing, learning, and lunch.
Prayer.
Helping one another.
Ask anything.

A typical morning

Specific times will vary from one daytime *Alpha Course* to another. It is important to allow enough time for small-group discussion after the talk and to make sure the schedule coordinates with local school times.

A schedule for daytime *Alpha* will look something like this:

9:45 A.M.	Child care opens
10:05 A.M.	Welcome & coffee
	Worship
10:35 A.M.	Announcements
10:40 A.M.	Talk
11:20 A.M.	Small Groups
12:00 P.M.	Child care ends

Values. The daytime *Alpha Course* promotes the same values as the evening *Alpha* with some small differences of emphasis, resulting from the time of the meeting and particularly from the ministry of "women to women." The main two values are:

- Lead the guests to a personal relationship with God through Jesus Christ.
- Love the lost, lonely, and unhappy.

Anyone may come, at any stage of their life and from any background. As with evening *Alpha* it is very important to make people feel welcome. Try to foster relationships in a relaxed atmosphere. Once during the ten weeks, plan lunch together as part of the course. It is very often a sign of the groups jelling together and friendships being formed when groups begin to arrange to have lunch together after the course is over.

Today many women take some kind of course in the morning—art, history, languages, etc.—so they can be encouraged to come and learn about the Christian faith. We also find that many, even those who are not Christians, have been crying out to God for their needs and those of their family (without knowing Him or His power to change things). As a consequence, they readily understand about prayer and begin to pray together early in the course.

The main difference in the organization and timing of daytime *Alpha* is the absence of the weekend away. It is often not practical for women to be separated from their families over an entire weekend. A good alternative is a day beginning with coffee at 9 A.M., followed by worship and a talk on "How Can I Be Filled with the Spirit?" which will combine three talks in one (chapters 8, 9, and 10 in *Questions of Life*). Include a time of ministry after the talk and then have lunch. Allow time for small groups where the guests can raise questions or the group can have time for more prayer. Make sure everything is over in time for moms to get their children after school.

Guests tend to enjoy the small groups more than anything else.

Small groups. Most guests tend to enjoy the small groups more than anything else. They often come needing love, acceptance, and forgiveness and they find it in their groups. Some come with damaged lives from abuse of all kinds. Many need a place of peace where they can learn to accept God's forgiveness for those things they have done of which they feel ashamed, and where they can learn to trust God and to forgive those who have hurt them. We try to group people of similar age and location together. Mothers enjoy being with others who have children of a similar age, as it means they all have similar joys and problems.

Daytime Alpha dinner. As with evening *Alpha*, hold a special Celebration Dinner. This dinner party at the end of the course is an excellent setting for married women to bring their husbands who oftentimes have been very pleasantly surprised at some of the changes in the lives of their spouses. The dinner gives husbands or other guests a wonderful opportunity to hear the Gospel in a relaxed environment. It has been one of the striking features of daytime *Alpha* that many of the husbands have gone on to do an evening *Alpha* and have come to know Christ. Women who are not married are encouraged to bring their friends to the dinner party.

Location. As with evening *Alpha*, daytime *Alpha* probably works best meeting in a home until the group gets too large. It can work very well in a church hall or similar building, providing there is room for child care.

Numbers. The course seems to work equally well whatever the numbers. We have done courses from twenty people to two hundred with the Lord working in equal power in people's lives.

Invitations and schedule. We suggest a letter or invitation card inviting people to join the morning *Alpha Course,* telling them how long the course is to run and the schedule of the morning. For example:

MORNING ALPHA

September 27th – December 6th
We invite you to join the new
Morning *Alpha* Course
beginning on
September 27th
The course runs for ten weeks on Wednesday mornings from
10:00 A.M. to 12 noon at (location). The mornings provide time
for a talk on Christian basics, followed by a break for coffee,
discussion groups, and an opportunity to ask questions. There will
be a special half-day with lunch on November 8th when the talk
will be "How Can I Be Filled with the Spirit?"
– further details later.

The course is ideal for anyone who wants to learn more about the
Christian faith and/or anyone who would like to inquire
into what Christianity really means. It is a wonderful
opportunity to meet new people and make new friends.
There are child care facilities if needed.

Team selection

Small-Group Leaders and Helpers. The priorities are the same as for an evening *Alpha:* choosing people who have vision for what the course can do, choosing new Christians who have many friends who do not know Christ, and training them to be helpers for the next course. It is possible to have smaller groups with the daytime *Alpha* (maybe eight or even six). There are two team members or leaders and one helper to each group.

Task Force. It is important to be well organized and to have someone from among the helpers who will organize the coffee for each morning, set out chairs, organize child care, and be responsible for arranging the lunch. There should also be a prayer task force who meet together for prayer half

It is important to be well organized.

an hour before the morning begins. All the team will be committed to praying, but with the various school starting times and other morning commitments it is not always possible for all the team to meet beforehand.

Ask the leaders and helpers to make the following commitments:
- Attend the entire course and all training.
- Be on time.
- Pray for all aspects of *Alpha* (the speaker, the small groups, the guests, etc.
- Prepare thoroughly for each session.

All leaders and helpers need to attend two training sessions: one before the course begins and one before the one-day retreat. The first session will cover Leading Small Groups and Pastoral Care (Tapes 3 & 4 of the *Alpha* Conference Tapes and Sessions 1 & 2 in the *Alpha* Leaders Training Video). The second training session will cover Ministry during *Alpha* (Tape 5 of the *Alpha Conference Tapes* or Session 3 of the *Alpha Leader Training Video*).

Results

During the years that we have had a daytime *Alpha*, we have had many wonderful conversions and healings. We have often found that after only a few weeks of the course whole families are coming to church.

AFTER ALPHA

In practice, the strong friendships often formed on *Alpha* mean that the small groups want to stay together afterward. However, new Christians need to be integrated into the life of the Christian community, and the appropriate ways of doing this will vary. With thousands of *Alpha Courses* now running, there have been many requests for more follow-up material suitable for use in a house group or small-group setting.

In response to this, we are compiling a program of adult Christian education which now includes the following:
- Term 1: *Questions of Life* (i.e., The *Alpha Course*)
- Term 2: *A Life Worth Living* (Nine studies in the Book of Philippians available in book and audiotape form)
- Term 3: *Searching Issues* (Seven studies on the most asked questions during *Alpha* in book and audiotape form)
- Terms 4 & 5: *Challenging Lifestyle* (Nineteen studies from the Sermon on the Mount)

These resources are described in more detail at the back of this book, their broad aim being to give people solid biblical roots for their new faith and lifestyle, and to address problems and difficult issues in a clear and simple way.

New Christians need to be integrated into . . . the Christian community.

Sometimes people ask me whether *Alpha* is always a success story. They want to know if every person who comes on the course becomes a Christian, is filled with the Spirit, gets excited about Jesus, and brings hundreds of friends to the next course. Unfortunately the answer is "No! It's not always like that!" We surveyed a recent course which had around four hundred guests and found that between sixty and eighty people dropped out. When we analyzed why, we found the following reasons.

First they stopped coming because of us. We did not run the course as well as we might have. For this reason we have questionnaires at the end of the course so that we can constantly improve it and make it more user-friendly. (See page 145 in this book for a reproducible copy of the *Alpha* Questionnaire.)

Secondly people drop out for good reasons. For example, some move to another part of the country. Increasingly, however, people are able to carry on the course where they move to. I know of one couple who started the course in London and finished it in Hong Kong. Another man did Weeks 1–7 at HTB, Week 8 in Boston, where he was on business, and then finished the course with us in London. This shows the advantage of the *Alpha* register (a listing of churches running *Alpha Courses* that appears in *Alpha News* three times per year).

Thirdly people drop out for reasons connected with the parable of the sower (Matthew 13:3-8 and 18-23). Jesus said that some people's hearts are hard: they are simply not ready to hear and they often leave after the first evening. Sometimes they come back on the next course or a year later. One person came back after four years and said to me, "I have never forgotten what I heard the first night."

Some drop out because of personal troubles in their lives, or through persecution or ridicule. Somebody may laugh at them and say, "What are you doing going to church on a Wednesday?" Many of the people who come on the course lie about what they are doing on Wednesday night. One man told me that a friend of his had come over from New Zealand and asked him out for a drink on a Wednesday night. Since he was going to *Alpha* he gave a vague excuse: he was not prepared to admit what he was doing. So his friend said, "Oh, that's a pity," and he looked through his calendar and said, "How about next Wednesday?" He explained that he was busy, but had difficulty justifying why he was busy the next Wednesday and the next. Finally he admitted to being on a course. "What course is that?" the friend asked. "Oh," he replied, "I am learning French." Many are not prepared to admit that they are taking a course about Christianity because they fear ridicule.

Jesus also outlines a third category of people for whom the cares of this world, the delight in riches, and the desire for other things come in and choke the Word. We've found that a relationship or success at work or some other distraction may take people away either during, or even after, the end of the course.

And that leaves the fourth category, which Jesus called the good soil. This bears fruit, thirtyfold, sixtyfold, or even a hundredfold. The minimum is thirtyfold. I was very encouraged by the second small group I lead. None of them were Christians but all of them came to Christ, were filled with the Spirit, and they are all now involved in the leadership of the church. I have kept in touch with all of them, except one. I had no idea what had happened to her until we went to Nairobi and ran an *Alpha* Conference. When we arrived, our host got us together in his house. I walked in and there was this girl called Nataya who I'm ashamed to say I didn't recognize. But as we walked into the room she started jumping up and down, a Masai way of showing excitement. She said that she had been praying for four years for *Alpha* to come to Kenya and she is now involved in running the course there. So all those people who came bore fruit: it was an amazing group. In the following group only one person stayed all the way through but she brought her husband and several of her friends to the next course. The seed that falls on good soil bears fruit thirtyfold, sixtyfold, a hundredfold.

4

Giving Talks

My message and my preaching were not with wise and persuasive words, but with a demonstration of the Spirit's power, so that your faith might not rest on men's wisdom, but on God's power.—1 Corinthians 2:4

Before I was a Christian, I was dragged to a talk which was one of a series in a mission at Cambridge. I remember looking at the clock at the start, determined not to listen, and watching it all the way through the talk, amazed at how long the speaker went on and how bored I was. Others seemed to be enjoying it and laughing. But I had told myself that I would not listen to a word of it.

When speaking to Christians, it is not unreasonable to assume an interest. We expect from the congregation a hunger to find out more about the Christian faith, to try to understand doctrine and study the Bible. With those who are not Christians we cannot make any such assumptions. Rather it is wise to assume they are asking, "Why should I listen?" and are challenging us to say something of interest to them.

We need to respond to this challenge. In the opening words, we have to tell them why they should listen. Truth in itself is not necessarily of interest. Truth is not the same as relevance. If we start by saying, "I want to expound the doctrine of justification by faith," then they are likely to fall asleep. However, if we begin with an attention-getting story or illustration

that introduces the topic, people will lean forward to catch every word. On the whole, people are not interested in theology or historical background until they see its relevance. We must arouse their interest right at the beginning: the first few seconds are vital.

They have got to think, "This is interesting. . . ." Like Jesus we need to begin with a need, a hurt, or something else of interest to the audience. Humor may be a way in, providing it leads us on to

I try to ensure that every such talk is centered on Jesus.

what we want to say. On the whole, people will listen to stories, whether they are humorous or serious. These should then lead into a subject of relevance to the hearers: work, stress, loneliness, relationships, marriage, family life, suffering, death, guilt, or fear.

In this chapter I want to look at the whole subject of speaking to nonchurchgoers (for example, those on *Alpha*) and in particular at giving an evangelistic talk (such as the *Alpha* Dinner at the end of the course). I believe it is a skill which many people could acquire. The major requirement is a strong desire to communicate the good news about Jesus Christ. In preparing such a talk there are seven vital questions we need to ask.

IS IT BIBLICAL?

The Bishop of Wakefield, the Rt. Rev. Nigel McCulloch, described a sermon, which he heard while he was on vacation, as a "disgrace." "The preacher spoke long, but said little. There was no message. As I looked around at my fellow-worshipers I could see from the sleeping of the old and the fidgeting of the young that they, like me, were finding the sermon dull, uninspiring, and irrelevant. What a lost opportunity. In fact, what a disgrace." He did not reveal the content of the sermon, but he did observe that "the congregation does not want third-rate personal comments on public affairs but real preaching that brings the Bible to life. . . . If St. Paul had been asked to advise the Church of England what to do in the Decade of Evangelism, he would tell us what he told Timothy. In every pulpit, in every church, at every service "preach the word."[1] This does not mean that talks to people who don't go to church must necessarily be biblical exposition. Rather they should be based on biblical truth and have verses of the Bible woven into their fabric.

In giving an evangelistic talk at the *Alpha* Dinner at the end of the course there are certain ingredients that I always try to include. Paul said that when he went to Corinth he "resolved to know nothing . . . except Jesus Christ and him crucified" (1 Corinthians 2:2). I try to ensure that every such talk is centered on Jesus. First, I say something about who He is, that Christianity is a historical faith based on the life, death, and resurrection of Jesus Christ, that the same Jesus is alive today, and that it is possible for us to have a relationship with Him. Secondly, I include something on "him crucified." I speak of what Jesus did on the cross when He died for us and how He made it possible for our sins to be forgiven and our guilt to be removed. Thirdly, I explain how someone can enter into a relationship with God, referring to repentance, faith, and receiving the Holy Spirit.

IS IT GOOD NEWS?

In His first sermon, Jesus chose to preach on the text from the prophet Isaiah, "The Spirit of the Lord is on me, because he has anointed me to preach good news to the poor" (Luke 4:18). Jesus did not come to condemn the world but to save it. The Gospel is good news in a world which is full of bad news. We should not simply make people feel guilty. We may need to talk about sin and guilt. But we do not want to leave people there. We are telling them about Jesus who frees us from sin, guilt, and evil. That is Good News!

 The Gospel is good news in a world which is full of bad news.

When Philip spoke to the Ethiopian eunuch he "told him the good news about Jesus" (Acts 8:35). I explain in the talk at the *Alpha* Dinner that Jesus Christ meets our deepest needs. I know that those listening who are not yet Christians will be struggling somewhere deep down with a lack of ultimate meaning and purpose in their lives; they will have no satisfactory answer to the inevitable fact of death or the universal problem of guilt. In all probability they will also be aware of a sense of "cosmic loneliness," a sense of being in God's world without the God for and by whom they were made.

Aware of these needs I try to show how Jesus dealt with our guilt on the cross, how He defeated death by His resurrection, how He made possible a relationship with God which gives meaning and purpose to life, and how He gives us His Holy Spirit so that we need never experience that cosmic loneliness. Of course, the good news of the kingdom of God includes far more than this. But in a twenty-minute talk at an *Alpha* Dinner I stick to a few very basic parts of this good news. Whenever I have finished writing a talk I ask myself the question, "Is this talk good news?"

IS IT INTERESTING?

We live in an age of TV, video games, and the Internet. People are not used to listening to long talks and it can be hard to retain their attention. Undiluted theology will not grip most people for very long. They prefer listening to stories and hearing how the point of those stories fits in with their lives. As a general rule, I find it helpful to follow the formula: point, illustration, application. If a talk has three points it will look something like this:

Introduction
I.   Point
    • Illustration
    • Application

II. Point
  • Illustration
  • Application
III. Point
  • Illustration
  • Application
Conclusion

It is worthwhile to collect illustrations. They come primarily from our own experience, but they can also come from newspapers, radio, TV, films, plays, books, and magazines. Of course, many of the best illustrations come from the Bible itself or from the natural world, and we need to think out carefully the applications for our listeners.

IS IT PERSUASIVE?

Paul tried "to persuade" people (2 Cor. 5:11). We need to work out what we are trying to achieve in a particular talk. For instance, are we trying to lead people to Christ, persuade them to start reading the Bible, or to pray? It is worth writing down the aim of a talk at the beginning. If we aim at nothing, we are likely to hit nothing. If we aim at too much, our efforts are likely to be dissipated. C. H. Spurgeon, the nineteenth-century preacher, said, "One tenpenny nail driven home and clenched will be more useful than a score of tin-tacks loosely fixed, to be pulled out again in an hour." [2]

Having established the aim, we need to ensure that every point is focused in that direction, like a tent supported from three or four different angles. We need to use every argument to appeal to the minds, hearts, and wills of the hearers.

There must be an appeal to the mind. We must give people reasons for doing what we are urging them to do. During the *Alpha Course* we try to teach all the basic elements of the Gospel. At an evangelistic *Alpha* Dinner we try to teach the crucial elements of the Good News.

If the talk were only appealing to the mind, it would be very dry. We need also to appeal to the heart. If, like me, you are British, you may find that hard. But people's emotions are involved as well. If it were purely an appeal to the emotions there would be a danger of emotionalism. Conversely, in appealing purely to the mind, we can stray into intellectualism.

Ultimately, if we are to persuade people to make a decision we need to appeal to their wills. In an evangelistic talk I try to drop a hint early on that there is a decision to be made, that there is no neutral ground, and there are no "don't knows" in the kingdom of God. I let them know what the options are. They can refuse Christ, accept Him, or just put off the decision. All this must be done without any pressure. It is right to persuade but wrong to pressurize.

IS IT PERSONAL?

Bishop Phillips Brooks of Boston, Massachusetts, defined preaching as "the bringing of truth through personality."[3] Of course, the message we want to get across is objectively true and much of what we say will be proclaiming that truth. However, it is a great help for the hearers if we can illustrate these truths from our own experience. We need to be honest and real, not pretending that we are perfect or that we never struggle in any areas of our lives. This does not mean that we have to make embarrassing public confessions, but it is helpful to acknowledge our own difficulties and failures. Stories told on ourselves can be both amusing and encouraging at the same time, provided they are set in a context which builds faith and are not purely negative. For example, I often tell stories about my early attempts at evangelism and the ridiculous things I did. I do it partly as a joke against myself, but also to assure people that we all make mistakes.

It is wise to talk generally in terms of "we" rather than "you." "You" can be very threatening and it suggests that we are somehow putting ourselves above our hearers. "We" is less threatening since it gives the impression that we are all in the same boat. "I" is the least threatening since it does not intimate that the hearers have the same problems: if it is used too frequently, the talk will appear self-centered. Generally, however, I would suggest that "you" and "I" should be used sparingly. "You" is often effective at the end of a talk: "What do you make of the claims of Christ?" "Will you decide today . . . ?"

IS IT UNDERSTANDABLE?

It is no use giving the greatest talk in the world if no one can understand it. It is often said that we should never overestimate an audience's knowledge and never underestimate their intelligence. Because knowledge is limited we need to avoid jargon (which is familiar only to the "in" crowd) and theological terms such as 'justification,' 'sanctification,' 'holiness,' 'atonement,' or any other word which is not used in everyday speech. The only case for using such words is if we explain in simple terms what we mean by them.

The other side of the coin is that because most people's intelligence is reasonably high, there is very little that they will not understand provided

It is right to persuade but wrong to pressurize.

It is no use giving the greatest talk in the world if no one can understand it.

it is clearly explained. Many theological books and talks are incomprehensible to most people, which is reasonable enough, if they are technical books for experts. However, I know for myself that if what I am saying gets very complicated, it is usually because I myself do not fully understand it. Albert Einstein once said, "You don't really understand something unless you can say it in a really simple way."

Certainly the teaching of Jesus was basically very simple. His economy in the Lord's Prayer, which comprises fifty-six words, is very favorable when compared to a recent European Union regulation report on the sale of cabbages which totals 26,901 words!

IS IT PRACTICAL?

The Bible often exhorts us to be "doers" rather than just "hearers." James writes, "Do not merely listen to the word, and so deceive yourselves. Do what it says" (Jas. 1:22). Jesus Himself said that what distinguished the wise man (who built his house upon a rock) from the foolish man (who built his house on sand) was that the wise man put into practice what he heard (Matt. 7:24), whereas the foolish man did not.

If we are to help people put into practice what they hear, then we need to be very practical. We need to show them how they can do what we are talking about. In an evangelistic talk we should explain carefully what a person needs to do if they want to give their life to Christ. The vital elements in the New Testament response seem to be repentance, faith, and receiving the Holy Spirit. I explain these using the words sorry, thank you, and please.

I explain repentance in terms of asking forgiveness for the past and turning away from everything we know to be wrong (that is "sorry"). I explain faith as putting our trust in what Jesus did for us on the Cross ("thank you") and I explain receiving the Spirit in terms of asking Him into our lives ("please"). Then I pray a prayer along the lines of the one in the booklet *Why Jesus?* and make it possible for the listeners to pray that prayer in their hearts along with me.

Finally, it is good to remember that it is more important to prepare ourselves than to be prepared in the technique of giving talks. Billy Graham, when speaking to 600 clergy in London in November 1979, said that if he had his ministry to do all over again he would make two changes. The audience looked rather startled. What could he mean? He said he would study three times as much as he had and he would give himself more to prayer. He quoted Dr. Donald Gray Barnhouse who said, "If I had only three years to serve the Lord, I would spend two of them studying and preparing."

TIP ON THE ALPHA TALKS

Because there are so many logistical details to beginning an *Alpha Course*, it may be easiest to use the video- or audiotapes to present the talks. Because these talks need to work for churches of all backgrounds and denominations, they are about an hour in length. As you develop live talks, you will want to adapt the material (especially the illustrations and stories) to fit your setting and situation. In doing so, you can shorten each talk to twenty or thirty minutes. To maintain a consistency among all *Alpha Courses* please do not change the essential character of the course. Consider moving to live talks gradually. With each successive course you can add two, three, or four live talks. While I present all of the prerecorded talks, in the live setting (at HTB in London) we feature a variety of speakers on each course. Different people identify more closely with different speakers. Therefore with a variety of speakers, the more likely it is that each guest will identify closely with one of them.

 Please do not change the essential character of the course.

5

Leading
Small Groups

Jesus said, "For where two or three come together in my name, there am I with them."—Matthew 18:20

John, a TV executive in his thirties, came with his wife, Tania, to an *Alpha* Dinner at the end of a course. Tania decided she wanted to attend the next course, but John agreed to come along only reluctantly. He played little part in the discussion groups, apart from the occasional, rather negative remark. On the weekend away he walked out of one of the sessions and told his wife they were leaving. She had become a Christian during the weekend and so was very disappointed. Nevertheless, she agreed to go with him. He told her on the way home that he was going to give up going to *Alpha*. I had not been involved in the weekend, but Tania told me on Sunday of John's decision. So on the following Wednesday I was amazed to see him walk through the door. Later in the evening, when we were in small groups, we went around the group, each person reporting on their experience of the weekend. When it came to John, he told us what had happened. Naturally, I asked him why he had come back. He replied simply, looking at the group, "I missed you a lot."

In John's case it was the small group which kept him coming to *Alpha*. He later gave his life to Jesus Christ and he and his wife are now firmly involved in the church. This incident shows us the vital importance of the small group.

AIMS

The overall purpose of the small group, along with the course as a whole, is to help to bring people into a relationship with Jesus Christ. Jesus Himself said that where two or three are gathered in His name He is there also (Matt. 18:20). We have found that a group of about 12 is the ideal size. I do not think it is a coincidence that Jesus chose a group of 12 (Mark 3:13-19). Within this overall purpose there are six subsidiary aims.

Give people the opportunity to respond to what they have heard.

AIM 1. TO DISCUSS THE TALK AND ISSUES ARISING OUT OF THE TALK

It is vital to give people the opportunity to respond to what they have heard and to ask questions. This is especially the case if the group is made up predominantly of those who are not yet Christians. Usually such groups are not ready to study the Bible. When we first ran *Alpha Courses,* the groups always studied the Bible from the first week. I soon realized that this was leading to considerable frustration. When the questionnaires came back at the end of the course there were comments such as, "I only really enjoyed our group when we were allowed to spend the whole time discussing the talk." Another wrote, "I would have liked more time discussing the talk and more freedom to diverge from the set Bible study."

Even if a Bible study is planned, it is important to give an opportunity to ask questions arising from the talk and to deal with these first. Otherwise, members of the group may feel frustrated that the real questions on their hearts and minds are not being answered.

Attend to practical details

The practical details are also very important. The chairs need to be arranged so that everyone is comfortable and can see one another. Light and ventilation need to be good. Everyone should have access to a modern translation of the Bible.

Good leadership involves many factors, including keeping to the set time. I discourage leaders from going on as a whole group beyond the scheduled time (9 P.M.) even if they are involved in a rip-roaring discussion. It is always possible to say, "Let's continue this next week," which will encourage them to return to continue the debate. If the groups go on too long people may be put off from coming back, fearing another late night.

Avoid two common errors

Some Bible studies are hampered by ineffective leadership where the leader is not in control. This may happen if the leader is not properly prepared or if he or she allows one person in the group to do all the talking.

Other Bible studies are ruined by an overly dominant leader who does all the talking, instead of giving others the freedom to speak and to say what is on their minds. The leader needs to be flexible enough to allow the group to change the subject, but confident enough to cut short gently any tangents that are frustrating the majority.

Ask simple questions

If the group is not ready for Bible study and discussion is not flowing very easily, there are possible discussion questions for each small-group time in *The Alpha Course Leader's Guide.* (See page 154 for ordering information.) There are two basic questions that usually work very well to get a discussion going:

- What do you think?
- What do you feel?

 By the end of *Alpha* people need to be able to study the Bible on their own.

Be prepared for possible common questions

I have found that some questions come up time and time again. The book *Searching Issues*[1] looks at the seven issues most often raised on *Alpha*. I encourage the leaders and helpers to be familiar with this material as well as to read about each of the subjects in it. The seven common issues include:

- Why does God allow suffering?
- What about other religions?
- Is there anything wrong with sex before marriage?
- How does the New Age movement compare to Christianity?
- What is the Christian attitude toward homosexuality?
- Is there a conflict between science and Christianity?
- Is the Trinity unbiblical, unbelievable, and irrelevant?

The leader needs to be prepared to lead the discussion and help bring out answers to the issues raised in the group.

AIM 2. TO MODEL BIBLE STUDY

Even though many groups are not ready for Bible study until after several weeks, the second aim of the small groups is to teach people how to read the Bible. There comes a point in most groups where it is appropriate to begin studying the Bible together. If most of the members of the group are Christians this may be the case right from the start. For the majority of the groups it will not be appropriate until later in the course, but it is important not to leave it too late. By the end of *Alpha* people need to be able to study the Bible on their own. It is the group Bible studies which give them both the enthusiasm to do this and the example of how it can be done.

The following suggestions have proven to be very effective in *Alpha* groups of all varieties.

If the leader wishes to open in prayer, it should be done sensitively. The leader may pray aloud or ask a member of the group to do so.

It is best . . . not to assume everyone is familiar with the Bible.

However, it needs to be done very carefully. People need to be asked beforehand and it needs to be made clear to the rest of the group that this is the case. Otherwise, they will be afraid that next time they may be asked to open in prayer.

If the group is ready for Bible study, the leader needs to prepare the passage carefully by reading the passage in different versions to gain an understanding of its meaning. The leader will try to spot any difficult verses and look up the explanation in a commentary (in order to avoid wasting time in the group). Next, it is important to explain carefully where the passage comes in the Bible and give the page number, so that no one is embarrassed by their lack of knowledge. People need to know it is okay to use the table of contents to locate a book of the Bible. Have a modern translation available for each guest. Sometimes it may be appropriate for each person to read a verse (for example, if the text is one of the psalms). This gets everyone involved. For some passages (e.g., the prodigal son) it is better for the whole passage to be read by one good reader. If there are difficult or unfamiliar words, the leader may read the passage aloud.

It is best for the leaders not to assume everyone is familiar with the Bible, its culture, style, layout, well-known stories, etc. Each leader should try to give a brief one- or two-sentence introduction to state the main theme of each passage. For example, when studying the story of the prodigal son, the leader might begin by saying, "Obviously, the father represents God and the son represents us. Let us see what lessons we can draw from the passage." The introduction must be very short and must not turn into a talk. It is a good moment to explain any obvious difficulties or ambiguous words. At all times leaders and helpers must avoid the use of spiritual clichés and Christian jargon that excludes non-Christians or new Christians.

Leaders should think of ways to provoke discussion of the passage and of key verses by avoiding questions that can be answered "yes" or "no." It is a good thing to work out the questions carefully. The aim is to bring everyone into the discussion. Contributions from the quieter members of the group should be especially welcomed. If one person has done a lot of talking, it is good to ask, "What do other people think?" Leaders need to try not to answer their own questions. Even if they are asked directly for a personal viewpoint, it is better, if possible, first to deflect the question.

It is important to avoid sounding patronizing at all costs. If the experience reminds the group of a lesson at school, they will feel most uncomfortable. The basic questions to ask about each passage are "What does it say?" "What does it mean?" and "How does it apply to our lives?" The aim is to help each person to discover both the meaning of the passage and the application to his or her daily life.

If a leader is asked questions he or she cannot answer, it is fatal to bluff. We need to admit we don't know all the answers. Such an admission is often seen as a strength rather than a weakness. The leader can always say he or she will make a note of the question and try to work on it for next time. This helps the learning process, both for guests and for leaders. It is important not to give the impression that there are easy answers to complicated questions or that the leaders or helpers are great experts. Everyone is learning together and the leaders are there to learn as much as to facilitate group study and discussion.

> **!** It is deeply moving to hear someone's first public prayer.

Aim 3. To model prayer

Thirdly, the small groups are the place to learn to pray as individuals and in a group. Again, this requires great sensitivity on the part of the Small-Group Leaders. Many, even if they are already Christians, are fearful of praying aloud. I know of one or two cases where people have stopped coming because they thought they might have to pray aloud. On the other hand, for those who do take the step and pray their first faltering prayer, it can be a momentous occasion, giving new confidence to their relationship with God. It is deeply moving to hear someone's first public prayer. It is usually completely uncluttered by jargon and obviously comes straight from the heart. It is good to make it clear to people that everyone benefits when they muster the courage to pray aloud, however briefly and simply.

Later on in the course it may be appropriate to end with prayer. As most people find praying out loud quite daunting in the initial stages, it is important to talk about these difficulties and then to model a very simple prayer, such as "Thank You for Your love. Amen." This will encourage others that they could do something similar. If a leader prays long eloquent prayers, others may be impressed but they will probably not pray themselves. If a simple model for prayer is provided, virtually everyone in the group prays, sometimes even those who are not yet Christians.

Before having someone pray aloud in the group, the leader needs to ask that person ahead of time. Then the leader can say to the group, "I have asked (person's name) to open (or close) in prayer."

Aim 4. To develop lasting friendships within the Body of Christ

John Wimber has often said, "People come to church for many reasons, but they stay for only one: that they make friends." We have found that extraordinarily close friendships are made in the course of ten weeks. Several years ago I had a small group of 12 people, none of whom were Christians at the start of the course, but by the end they had all come to faith in Christ. All are now in positions of Christian leadership and remain

It is impossible to exaggerate the importance of prayer.

very close. Immediately after the course, one of them said that before it had begun he had felt his "friends' register" was full and was amazed to find that he had made so many lasting relationships.

AIM 5. TO LEARN TO MINISTER TO ONE ANOTHER

The small group is the place for those on the course to learn to minister to one another in the power of the Holy Spirit. The small group in which I was involved during a recent course started out full of questions, some of which were quite hostile. The group members all seemed so different that I began to wonder whether they would all get along with each other. But by the end it was wonderful to see them all praying for each other, laying on hands, and praying for healing. It is often in the context of the small group that people are able to discover and use their spiritual gifts.

AIM 6. TO TRAIN HELPERS TO LEAD NEXT TIME

Finally, one of the aims of the Small-Group Leader is to train others to lead. *Alpha* has grown at such a rate that at HTB we continually need more leaders. It has grown from one small group to thirty-four small groups on the current *Alpha Course*. Initially the leaders were experienced Christians, often of at least ten years' standing. Many of the helpers these days have become Christians on the previous *Alpha Course* and even the leaders may have been Christians for as little as six months. This is not ideal, but it is a good problem to have: presumably the early church was faced with a similar situation. When 3,000 were converted on the Day of Pentecost, some of them must have needed to lead virtually straightaway.

SECRETS OF SUCCESS

PRAYER

For the leader or helper on *Alpha* it is impossible to exaggerate the importance of prayer. At the prayer meeting before every weekly session of the course we pray about the worship, the talk, the small groups, the general atmosphere, the administration, the weekend, and the dinner party(ies) at the end. In addition I ask them to pray for those in their small groups as often as they can. There seems to be a direct correlation between the amount of prayer and the fruitfulness of the small groups. Groups which have borne lasting fruit have always had at least one helper who was strongly committed to praying for each member of the group.

PERSONAL CARING

The leaders and helpers need to get to know each person in the group. It is important to learn their names on the first night. Sometimes we play a name game to make this easier. Each evening of the course the group sits together for supper and the leaders and helpers act as hosts and facilitate the conversations. Sometimes the group will go out together at the end of the evening. Sometimes they will meet up during the week, either on a one-to-one basis or as a group with everyone together.

People need to feel it is safe to raise their honest questions.

ENCOURAGEMENT

A good leader will always be an encourager. At the most basic level this means smiling at people, being interested in what each person has to say, and showing an interest in each person. It is important to give everyone an opportunity to ask questions about the talk. People need to feel it is safe to raise their honest questions.

COMMITMENT

On the evenings themselves it is important for the helpers and leaders of each group to get together to talk and pray for their group and also to discuss the ways of overcoming any problems within it. It is essential that the *Alpha* Team consistently attend all sessions and the weekend away. In this way, the team subtly emphasizes the importance of the course.

6

Pastoral Care

"We proclaim him, admonishing and teaching everyone with all wisdom, so that we may present everyone perfect in Christ. To this end I labor, struggling with all his energy, which so powerfully works in me."—Colossians 1:28-29

The first words of Jesus to Peter (in Mark's Gospel) were: "Come, follow me . . . and I will make you fishers of men" (Mark 1:17). In His last conversation with Peter (in John's Gospel) Jesus repeated, "Follow me!" (John 21:19) and urged Peter to feed and take care of the sheep and the lambs. The first priority is our relationship with Jesus. The second is our relationship with others.

In this last recorded conversation with Jesus on earth, Peter tells Jesus three times that he loves Him. Each time Jesus' response is to tell Peter to look after other people. If we love Jesus, we will make this a high priority in our lives. Indeed it is part of following Jesus' example. He had compassion on people and once compared His longing to care for them and look after them to a hen with her chicks (Luke 13:34).

King David was a man who had experience with pastoral care as a shepherd tending sheep and also in the sense of being a shepherd of God's people. The psalmist says that "David shepherded them with integrity of heart; with skillful hands he led them" (Ps. 78:72). Pastoral care involves our hearts and our hands. We must have an integrity of heart: our love for people and our friendship with them must be genuine. There must be no false pretense. This love needs to be combined with "skillful hands." There are skills which we can learn. Obviously in a short chapter we cannot look at all the skills of pastoral care but I want to mention some of the general principles involved in this area.

AIMS

Paul's aim was to "present everyone perfect in Christ" (Col. 1:28). Some versions translate the word for perfect as "mature." Perfection is not something we can reach in this life, but it is possible to become mature. Three vital points emerge from this verse.

On *Alpha* . . . every single person should be looked after.

AIM 1: TO MINISTER TO ALL PARTICIPANTS

First, Paul's concern is for everyone. A good pastor will not want to lose any of his sheep. The aim on *Alpha* is that every single person should be looked after, which is why each group has two main leaders and two helpers. The idea is that one of the leaders or helpers takes responsibility for each of the members in the group. It is a flexible and very relaxed system but the clear aim is that everyone on the course should receive care and prayer.

This system of one-to-one care is perhaps the most crucial aspect of *Alpha*. For myself, I owe so much to the man who helped me on an individual basis, early in my Christian life. He sacrificed his time to answer my questions, explain the Christian faith to me, and give me advice, guidance, and friendship. It was always fun to be with him: indeed, it was the highlight of my week as he helped me to lay the foundations of my Christian life.

Care like this is much more likely to meet people's needs. Preaching and teaching are inevitably like throwing a bucket of water over empty bottles, whereas one-to-one pastoral care is like filling each bottle individually from the faucet. Not only is it the most effective method, it is also a form of Christian service in which everyone can take part as it does not require great speaking or leadership gifts.

Juan Carlos Ortiz tells the story of meeting an elderly lady in his native Argentina. She introduced him to a young girl who was one of her great-grandchildren. She went on to tell him that she had six children and thirty-six grandchildren. Her family was impressive in number and among her grandchildren were many well-educated and professional people. Ortiz asked her, "How did you manage to produce such a large, well-fed, well-dressed, well-educated, extended family?" She replied, "I didn't. I just took care of the six and each of them took care of their six."[1]

Preachers can overestimate the amount of truth that is assimilated between the pulpit and the pew. Bill Hybels and Don Cousins, leaders of the 19,000-strong Willow Creek Community Church near Chicago, have spoken about their experiences of coming to realize that sermons in and of themselves do not prepare people to live effective Christian lives. Hybels states that every major strategic step or decision he has made was inspired and encouraged by someone three feet from him and not in a crowd of a thousand people. "Truth applied across a table" has been a key to his own personal growth.

AIM 2: TO BRING EACH PERSON TO SPIRITUAL MATURITY

Secondly, our aim in this one-to-one pastoral care is spiritual maturity. Of course, this cannot happen overnight or even during a ten-week course. The leaders' and helpers' aim is to assist people through the early stages and then integrate them into a group within the life of the church where they can grow and mature further.

 We do not want to attach people to ourselves but to Christ.

At HTB the groups on *Alpha* are arranged, right from the start, with this express aim. That is why, ideally, the team in each small group should come from the same home group and at least one of the leaders or helpers should go with the group back to that home group and help introduce and integrate the new members. If your church does not have home groups, perhaps you have other small groups or adult classes on Sunday mornings, Wednesday evenings, or other times. Whatever your structure, the important thing is to have a means to extend people's involvement with the church beyond *Alpha*.

AIM 3: TO ENCOURAGE EACH PERSON TO SEEK CHRIST

Thirdly, Paul's aim is maturity in Christ. We do not want to attach people to ourselves but to Christ. Good parents encourage independence in their children. They begin by feeding their children, but teach them, as soon as possible, to feed themselves. We need to beware of any unhealthy dependence on us and help people to become dependent on Christ.

Our aim is that every person who comes to *Alpha* should come to spiritual maturity in Christ. In practice, of course, a number of people drop out. Our surveys have shown that about 20 percent do not complete the course. Half of these people drop out for good reasons, such as moving away.

Some drop out the first night and we often do not know the reason why. Others leave because of the teaching—for example, teaching the biblical view on sex before marriage. Others find friends laugh at them for going to church and they are put off for that reason. For others still it is "the worries of this life, the deceitfulness of wealth and the desires for other things" (Mark 4:19).

As in the parable of the sower, those for whom the seed falls on good soil "hear the word, accept it, and produce a crop—thirty, sixty or even a hundred times what was sown" (Mark 4:20). That is why we find that however many people drop out, the next course is almost invariably larger than the one before.

People need to grow in their relationships within the Body of Christ.

METHOD

Paul's method was to proclaim Christ. He wrote, "We proclaim him, admonishing and teaching everyone with all wisdom" (Col. 1:28). Jesus Christ is the key to spiritual maturity. We grow in maturity as our knowledge of Him and intimacy with Him grow.

LEAD PEOPLE TO JESUS

Many of those who attend an *Alpha Course* are not yet Christians. The aim is to lead them to Christ. They may give their lives to Christ during one of the main sessions or they may do it on their own. But every leader and helper should know how to lead someone into a relationship with Christ. *Why Jesus?* is the booklet we use on *Alpha* as a resource in this area. I use it myself when explaining the Christian faith to those who are not Christians and then I encourage them to pray the prayer in the back of the booklet. Sometimes they will want to pray it on their own, but more often they would prefer to pray it out loud with someone. There is also a Christmas version called *Why Christmas?*

ENCOURAGE NEW CHRISTIANS TO GROW IN THEIR RELATIONSHIP WITH JESUS

Once people have come to Christ, it is vital to encourage them to grow in that relationship. Bible reading and prayer are the keys to this. We need to help them with reading the Bible and advise them as to how they might pray on their own. We can give practical advice about which translation of the Bible might be appropriate to buy and guide them toward some suitable Bible reading notes. And it is good to explain that Bible reading is not an end in itself but a means of experiencing a relationship with Jesus Christ (John 5:39-40).

In addition to the Bible, Christian books can be a great help. We encourage people to read a balanced diet of doctrinal, biographical, and devotional books. Some are not great readers and prefer to listen to tapes of the *Alpha* talks and other subjects. Many people enjoy listening to them in the car or when working or relaxing around the home and this reinforces their faith.

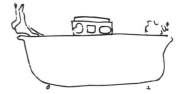

ENCOURAGE NEW CHRISTIANS TO GROW IN THEIR RELATIONSHIPS WITHIN THE BODY OF CHRIST

In order to become mature in Christ, people need to grow in their relationships within the Body of Christ. The small group is the ideal place to start developing such friendships. As weekly meetings proceed, friendships grow quite naturally. We can encourage the process by acting as a catalyst for discussion in the early stages, when people don't know each other well. Later, if they start coming to church for Sunday worship or other regular meetings, it can help if group members arrange to meet and sit together. If any of them live near each other, sharing rides encourages both the person who is driving and the person who is riding to come regularly.

People . . . thrive in an atmosphere of love and encouragement.

ATTITUDE

In helping the people who attend *Alpha* to grow into maturity in Christ, we have found three principles to be of great importance:

ENCOURAGER

In his early Christian life, Paul was much encouraged by Barnabas. He in turn became a great encourager (Acts 16:40; 20:1-2). He also wrote urging Christians to "encourage one another and build each other up" (1 Thess. 5:11). In the world there is so much negative criticism, leading all too often to insecurity and timidity. People shrivel up emotionally in an atmosphere of criticism, and they thrive in an atmosphere of love and encouragement. We need to express warmth and responsiveness to those who are searching or are new Christians.

LISTENER

James writes, "Everyone should be quick to listen, slow to speak . . . " (Jas. 1:19). It is the task of the *Alpha* Team to draw out the guests and listen to them. Everyone on the team should take a genuine interest in the guests and encourage them to speak about themselves. If guests have ideas which are contrary to the Christian faith, leaders or helpers should not be quick to correct them. Instead, the leaders need to listen, to try to understand where the other person is coming from, and to show respect for people even if they disagree totally with their ideas. If the guests reach a point where they are interested and intrigued enough to ask what someone on the *Alpha* Team thinks, they will pay far more attention to what is said.

Helping on *Alpha* involves a commitment to pray.

PEACEMAKER

Jesus said, "Blessed are the peacemakers" (Matt. 5:9). It is important for the *Alpha* Team to be gracious and courteous and to avoid getting involved in arguments.

"...But the Hebrew for love is..."

On the whole, people will not be convinced if they get involved in an argument, especially if it is in front of others in the group. They tend to dig in their heels, which makes it harder for them to give up their position later if they wish to do so. It is easy to win an argument and lose a person. If there is an argument brewing, the leader should try to reconcile differences and relieve tension, diplomatically exploring reasons for the differences. Usually there will be an element of truth in both points of view and the leader can say, "Isn't it a bit of both? Fred is right in saying . . . and George is right in saying. . . ." Then both Fred and George feel affirmed and the argument is over. Obviously, truth is what matters but the truth needs to be spoken in love and we need to be careful that "speaking the truth" is not an excuse for a personality clash, an expression of anger, or a wrong exertion of authority.

COMMITMENT

Paul says, "To this end I labor, struggling with all his energy, which so powerfully works in me" (Col. 1:29). In Paul's pastoral care there was a balance between God's grace and his own responsibility. Our pastoral care should express the same balance. There is an element of "toiling" and "striving" involved in all effective Christian ministry.

OUR RESPONSIBILITY

Being a part of the *Alpha* leadership team involves a great deal of hard work. It requires a high level of commitment. Guests on *Alpha* are unlikely to reach a higher level of commitment than the leaders and helpers in their group. If the team does not attend regularly, those attending *Alpha* are unlikely to do so. I ask leaders and helpers to block out on their calendars all the evenings of the training course, as well as the 10 Wednesdays of the course, the Celebration Dinner at the end, and the weekend. Of course, occasions will arise when they are unable to attend, because they are out of town, required to work, or ill. But I ask them to give *Alpha* the same priority they would give to their job.

This commitment is necessary because there are times when it will be a real effort to get there and talk to people until quite late at night sometimes. It requires an effort to talk to new people, rather than talking to friends. I ask the team to pray and prepare beforehand so that when they are there they can concentrate all their efforts on the guests. This kind of effort makes for a very long evening.

Most important of all, helping on *Alpha* involves a commitment to pray. We ask the team to come to the prayer meeting every Wednesday, if they can possibly get away from work in time. We also ask them to commit themselves to praying regularly for every aspect of *Alpha:* the worship, talks, ministry, and administration, as well as praying daily, if they can, for the individual members of their group.

 I encourage all the team to receive from the Lord.

GOD'S GRACE

The other side of our responsibility is God's grace. We do not "labor" and "struggle" on our own. We do it "with all his energy, which so powerfully works" in us (Col. 1:29). We need His help and His power for every task. When the disciples chose people to wait on tables, they chose those who were "full of the Spirit and wisdom" (Acts 6:3).

I encourage all the team to receive from the Lord, both at the prayer meeting beforehand and during the main session, as they enter into the worship and listen to the talk. Even if they have heard the talk several times before, they can pray that God will show them something new and relevant to their lives. All the time I encourage them to pray for God to fill them with His Spirit and empower them with all the gifts they need: evangelism, teaching, pastoring, and prophecy (the ability to hear what God is saying in a specific situation and pass it on to others).

It is this individual one-to-one pastoral care which is one of the most exciting aspects of *Alpha*. Members of the team often tell me thrilling stories about what has happened to an individual during the course. Not only has that individual's life been changed but it has brought great blessing to the member of the team who befriended him or her. There is no greater joy than to lead someone to Christ and watch that person begin to grow in the faith.

The nineteenth-century evangelist R. A. Torrey, writing on the subject of pastoral care, said he believed that when the membership of any local church exercised its responsibility and privilege in this matter, and each and every member of church acted it out in the power of the Holy Spirit, "a great revival will be close at hand for the community in which that local church is located. [It] is a work that wins but little applause from men, but it accomplishes great things for God."[2]

7

Ministry

"All this is from God, who reconciled us to himself through Christ and gave us the ministry of reconciliation."—2 Corinthians 5:18

What makes *Alpha* so exciting is the work of the Holy Spirit among us. It is His activity which transforms the talks, the discussion groups, the Bible studies, pastoral care, administration, and every other aspect of *Alpha*. The word "ministry" is used in several different ways in the New Testament and in the church today. In one sense, ministry includes everything done in a church and every aspect of an *Alpha Course*. John Wimber has defined ministry as "meeting the needs of others on the basis of God's resources." *The New Bible Dictionary* points out, "In its earliest form the Christian ministry is charismatic, i.e., it is a spiritual gift or supernatural endowment, whose exercise witnesses to the presence of the Holy Spirit in the Church."[1] In this chapter, however, I am using a narrower sense of the word: when we specifically pray for others in the power of the Holy Spirit.

One of the most astonishing stories in the Old Testament is the account of Moses and the people of Israel crossing the Red Sea. When they came to the sea God said to Moses, "Raise your staff and stretch out your hand over the sea to divide the water so that the Israelites can go through the sea on dry ground" (Exod. 14:16). God was asking Moses to do his part while promising to do His own part, by dividing the sea. I wonder what went through Moses' mind at that moment. He would have felt a fool if he had stretched out his hand and God had not divided the sea. He may have thought it would have been much easier if God had just divided the sea without involving him. But as is often the case in the Bible, there is a cooperation between us and God. God allows us to be involved in His plans. We do our part and God does His. Our part is relatively simple. God's is not so easy.

Moses took a step of faith and "stretched out his hand" (14:21). God responded and " . . . all that night the Lord drove the sea back with a strong east wind and turned it into dry land. The waters were divided, and the Israelites went through the sea on dry ground, with a wall of water on their right and on their left" (vss. 21-22).

We are to keep looking to Jesus.

God has not changed. This story reminds us that when we do what He asks us to do, He does what He has promised to do. As we pray for others He sends His Holy Spirit to transform lives. This might be prayer for others to be filled with the Spirit, to receive some gift (for example, the gift of tongues), or prayer for healing.

VALUES FOR MINISTRY

MINISTRY OF THE HOLY SPIRIT

The most fundamental thing here is to recognize that this is a ministry of the Holy Spirit. It is not our power but His. What God asked Moses to do was very simple; he did not have to shout or dance or leap about. Likewise, we encourage our leaders to be totally natural and simply to be themselves, to take a step of faith and stretch out their hands, and to ask God to send His Spirit. The rest is up to Him. Sometimes I look around while ministry is happening and see leaders or helpers stepping out in faith for the first time in this area. There is often an expression of astonishment, bewilderment, and joy on their faces as they see how God uses them.

Sometimes when we see the extraordinary work of the Spirit we may be tempted to look at the fruit rather than the vine. But we are to keep looking to Jesus. Jesus taught His disciples not to be sidetracked in any way from the most important issues. When the seventy-two returned joyfully from the places they had been sent to minister to and said, "Lord, even the demons submit to us in your name" (Luke 10:17), Jesus replied, "I saw Satan fall like lightning from heaven. I have given you authority to trample on snakes and scorpions and to overcome all the power of the enemy; nothing will harm you. However, do not rejoice that the spirits submit to you, but rejoice that your names are written in heaven" (vss. 18-20).

AUTHORITY OF THE BIBLE

Second, and of equal importance, all ministry must take place under the authority of the Bible. The Spirit of God and the written word of God will never be in conflict. They complement each other. God will never do or say anything which is inconsistent with His revealed will and character in the Bible. Because the Word and the Spirit go hand in hand we encourage our leaders to be steeped in the biblical truths and promises as part of ministry. It is the truth that sets people free (John 8:32). I ask people to make sure they know where key passages are that relate to the kinds of needs which emerge as we pray for people. For example, some of the passages we often use are the following:

Psalm 51	Repentance
Psalm 91	Fear
Philippians 4:6-7	Anxiety
Psalm 37:5	Guidance
1 Corinthians 10:13	Temptation

If we love people we will show them respect.

DIGNITY OF THE INDIVIDUAL

Our third main concern in ministry is the dignity of the individual: if we love people we will show them respect. This means first that confidentiality is assured. If people tell us some confidential matter about their lives, they need to be assured it will go no further. It will not be "shared for prayer" or discussed at helpers' meetings. Next, we must affirm rather than condemn. We don't say, "It's your fault" or "You don't have enough faith" if people are not healed. Jesus never told an individual that it was their lack of faith that stopped them from being healed. Occasionally He upbraided His disciples for their lack of faith (and we may need to ask ourselves whether we lack faith) but He never condemned the sick person in this way. We should not place additional burdens on anyone, let alone those who are sick. If they are not healed, we never suggest that they should believe that they are. Rather, we give them the freedom to come back and pray again. This kind of prayer should always be done in a low-key way and any super-spirituality and unnatural intensity should be avoided at all costs.

HARMONY OF RELATIONSHIPS

The fourth value is harmonious relationships. Jesus prayed for His disciples, "May they be brought to complete unity to let the world know that you sent me and have loved them even as you have loved me" (John 17:23). The unity of the people of God was a high priority on Jesus' agenda and it should be so on ours. A lack of unity, love, and forgiveness on the team hinders the work of the Spirit and is a terrible example to those on *Alpha*. It is vital that each group's leaders and helpers find time to pray together, as prayer is the most effective way of rooting out petty irritations. We make it a rule on *Alpha* never to criticize another denomination, another Christian church, or a Christian leader. We try to support and encourage one another constantly. I discourage anyone from making negative remarks about another team member even as a joke. We are extremely careful during the entertainment on the weekend away not to allow any skits which have even a hint of cynicism or are in any way negative. This may seem excessive, but we have found in the past that even the most off-the-cuff comment can have a detrimental effect.

THE BODY OF CHRIST

The fifth value of *Alpha* is the vital importance of the Body of Christ. The Christian community is the place where long-term healing and spiritual growth take place under the protective umbrella of the authority of the church. Hence, we stress that each person should try to find a group where they can grow and develop. Leaders and helpers are responsible for helping each person under their care to find such a group.

A MODEL FOR MINISTRY

As well as having values on which our ministry is based, it is important to have a model about which we are confident so that all the theory may be put into practice and not left simply as theory. Over the years with *Alpha* we have developed a model which is not the only way or even necessarily the best way, but it is one which we have found God works through and is simple enough for anyone to use and to feel confident in doing so.

TEAM PRAYER

When praying for individuals, ideally do so with a team of two or, at most, three. Sometimes, for example, on the Sunday morning of the weekend on the Holy Spirit, there are so many people who want to be prayed for that there are not enough leaders and helpers to go around. On these occasions there may be only one person praying for each individual. If this is the case, make it an absolute rule that men should pray for men and women for women. Often during these times of prayer the Holy Spirit brings out aspects of people's lives which are very personal and intimate. Also, at these moments a very strong bond may be formed between the person praying and the one being prayed for, and if the person is of the opposite sex there is a danger of misunderstanding and a misreading of signals. If there is more than one person praying, then at least one should be of the same sex as the person being prayed for.

PRAYER LEADER

At these prayer times one person should take the lead and should be seen to do so with the prayerful help of the others. If more than one person is attempting to lead there is a danger that signals will be confused. For example, it is not helpful if one is saying, "Hold on," and the other is saying, "Let go!"

One person should take the lead.

As far as possible it is good to find a relaxed and private place to pray. If there are a lot of people in the room, it is important that others around cannot hear everything that is being said, to avoid embarrassment for the person receiving prayer. It is unnecessary and even inappropriate to raise one's voice or to shout during prayer. Such behavior can be intensely uncomfortable for the person receiving prayer and for other guests.

 It is good to find a relaxed and private place to pray.

DIFFICULTIES

We usually begin by asking the person what they would like prayer for. We then take time to sort out difficulties in understanding, belief, and assurance. Often there is a need for repentance and forgiveness, both receiving and offering forgiveness. Lack of repentance and forgiveness are major stumbling blocks to the work of the Holy Spirit in our lives.

Sometimes at this point it becomes clear that the person is not yet a Christian. All members of the team need to be confident that they can lead someone to Christ. I would usually go through the booklet *Why Jesus?* briefly and then ask the person if he or she would like to pray the prayer in the back right then or later when there has been time to think about it. It is important always to give people an out which is equally acceptable so that they do not feel pressured into doing something for which they are not ready. If the person says, "Yes, I would like to do so right now," I would pray briefly and then encourage that person to read the prayer out loud, slowly and thoughtfully, adding anything he or she wishes. After this I would pray another prayer for them asking the Spirit of God to come and fill him or her.

Others may already be Christians but have never really experienced God or the power of the Holy Spirit. Encourage these with truth through scriptural illustrations and promises. Be sensitive to deal with any difficulties they may have. Some may say, "Am I quite ready?" to which the answer, in one sense, is that we will never be totally ready. Some say, "I'm unworthy," to which the answer is, "We are all unworthy. That is why Jesus died for us." Most often there is a feeling that it could "never happen to me." For example, one might want to receive the gift of tongues but say, "I could never speak in another language." Again, raise faith by pointing to the promises of God (1 Cor. 14:2, 4, 14; Matt. 7:11). One aspect of faith is taking a promise of God and daring to believe it.

PRAYER

As we pray for people, we stay facing them and if they have no objection, we lay hands on them. Then, keeping our eyes open, we ask the Holy

We encourage the people to hold on to the promises of God.

Spirit to come. We welcome Him when we see signs of His working and wait on God as we pray for further directions. It is important not to pray "around-the-world" prayers or to go off in every conceivable direction because you are running out of things to pray for. Rather, we silently ask God what He wants to do or say, how He wants to encourage the person, and what gifts He wants to impart.

On the *Alpha* weekend we often pray for people to receive the gift of tongues (see *Questions of Life*, pages 155-163). This is not because it is the most important gift but because the *Alpha Course* is a beginner's course and the gift of tongues is a beginner's gift. It is neither the mark of being a Christian, nor a necessary sign of being filled with the Spirit. The gift of tongues does not elevate you into a spiritual elite, nor is it indeed necessary to speak in tongues. However, both in the Bible and in experience it is often the first obviously supernatural gift of the Spirit which people receive. Our understanding of the New Testament is that it is available to all Christians and therefore we can pray with great confidence for them to receive it.

The small group is the place to deal with people's fears and hesitations. I would ask those in the small group if anyone has had any experience in this area, good or bad. If they have, I ask them to speak about it. Usually there is someone (it might be a leader or a helper) who speaks in tongues and is able to explain what it is and what the benefits are.

When praying for people to receive the gift of tongues, I have found the greatest barrier is a psychological one—making the first sound. Once a person has made the first sound the rest usually follows quite naturally. In order to help people to get over this barrier I explain this difficulty and suggest that they start by repeating what I or one of the other ministry team members is saying. Then I start to speak in tongues slowly so that they can follow. Once they have made the first sound they are usually away praying in their own language. I encourage them to try to concentrate on their relationship with God and try, as far as possible, not to be self-conscious. Rather they should concentrate on praising God with the new language He has given to them.

INTERACTION

After we have finished praying for people to be filled with the Spirit, receive a gift, be healed, or whatever it is, we ask what is happening and what they sense God is saying to them. We encourage the people to hold on to the promises of God, and warn them against possible increased temptation. We don't believe it is possible that "nothing has happened."

People may not be aware especially at the time but when we ask the Spirit of God to come, He has promised to come. They may not know the difference until hours or even days later, but something will have happened. We need to encourage all people to keep in touch and to let us know how they are getting on. Of course, it is not a onetime experience; they need to go on being filled with the Spirit (Eph. 5:18).

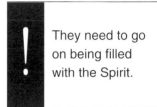

They need to go on being filled with the Spirit.

OPPORTUNITIES FOR MINISTRY

Weekend retreat

Much of the ministry takes place on the weekend away. The early part of the weekend is usually spent in raising faith and dealing with difficulties. On Friday night we have a very short talk on the Holy Spirit based around John 15:26. I try to keep this short and lighthearted as people are often exhausted after a busy week and a long journey.

On the Saturday morning we look at "Who Is the Holy Spirit?" and "What Does the Holy Spirit Do?" (see *Questions of Life*, chapters 8 and 9). Then we go into the usual small groups and look at 1 Corinthians 12:1-8. This gives people an opportunity to discuss some of the most obviously supernatural gifts of the Spirit.

On Saturday afternoon there is an opportunity to ask for counseling with an experienced (though not professionally trained) counselor. We put up a list of the counselors and people can sign up for this if they have questions they want to ask, difficulties they would like help in thinking through, or some area in their lives where they would like to receive prayer. During these sessions some give their lives to Christ, some are filled with the Spirit, and others receive new gifts.

On the Saturday evening I speak on "How Can I Be Filled with the Spirit?" (chapter 10 in *Questions of Life*). At the end of the talk I explain that I am going to invite the Holy Spirit to come and fill those who would like to be filled and to give the gift of tongues to those who would like to receive. I ask everyone to stand, to close their eyes, and to hold out their hands in front of them if they would like to receive. Our body language often expresses what we feel, and holding out our hands is what we do when we are about to receive a gift: thus it is a sign between the people and God that they would like to receive from Him.

I then pray a prayer which others can echo in their hearts. It is a prayer of repentance, faith, and commitment to Jesus Christ. Then I ask the Holy Spirit to come and fill all those who have invited Him into their lives. We then wait and watch as He comes and does what He wants to do. It is

We then wait and watch as He comes.

always different and always exciting to see God at work in our midst. Sometimes the manifestations of the Spirit are obvious. Some are so overwhelmed by the Holy Spirit they find it hard to remain standing. Others are so deeply moved by the love of God that tears run down their faces. Some are so filled with joy that they burst out laughing. For others there is no outward manifestation, but a work of God in their hearts brings a sense of peace and a deep assurance of His presence and love. All should be encouraged, and no one should be made to feel guilty, second-rate, or rushed along against his or her will.

At the end of the course I send out questionnaires asking whether people were Christians before the course and how they would describe themselves now. If there is a change, I ask when that change occurred. For many the decisive moment is the Saturday evening of the weekend. Here are five examples of how people at one *Alpha* weekend described their experiences:

• After the talk about "How Can I Be Filled with the Spirit?" we all stood up and the Holy Spirit came into the room. I knew that God was real so I asked Jesus into my heart and He's been there ever since. . . . I have suddenly got a whole new outlook on life.

• The change had occurred during the Saturday evening talks/services. I was filled with the Holy Spirit. I felt a white sheet wipe me clean then a strong rush of light came through me from my waist and up out of my head—the feeling made me lift my arms in the air.

• I had been a Christian in my head only. This changed on the *Alpha* weekend when God spoke to me personally. I asked Him for His Holy Spirit and the result was electrifying.

• Someone who had been involved in the New Age movement at the start of the course said that the change occurred on the Saturday evening when "the Spirit shook me from head to foot."

• I had a phenomenal experience of the Holy Spirit cleansing me, freeing me, releasing my sins and loving me; giving me a fresh plateau, a new life. It was the 20th [of] February when I really started to live!

After the Saturday evening we respond to God in songs of thanksgiving and praise. Sometimes we will sing in tongues. I explain that singing in tongues together is different from all speaking in tongues together.

Speaking in tongues without interpretation is a private activity which should only be done on our own. Singing in tongues is a corporate activity of praise and worship to God, coordinated by the Spirit of God. On occasions, it has been one of the most beautiful and almost angelic sounds I have ever heard. It is also a golden opportunity for people to receive the gift of tongues as they begin to sing praises to God in the language He gives them.

 We respond by giving ourselves to Him out of love.

We do not usually pray for individuals on the Saturday night unless they specifically ask for prayer (which some often do at this stage). Instead, after dinner we have an evening of entertainment organized by someone on the team. This is a good time for people to relax and unwind by performing or watching. We invite participation by anyone who would like to contribute. It is usually a mixture of musical contributions, joke telling, and amusing skits. The quality is sometimes a little mixed, but it always involves lots of laughter. We try to ensure that the whole evening is as positive and edifying as possible.

On Sunday morning we meet in small groups briefly to make sure that everyone is doing well and to discuss any difficulties or questions which may have arisen on the Saturday. Then we have our informal communion service. We begin with praise and prayer. Then we have a talk on "How Can I Make the Most of the Rest of My Life?" (see *Questions of Life*, chapter 15). At the end I invite people to give every part of their lives to God, "to offer your bodies as living sacrifices" (Rom. 12:1). This is the appropriate response to all that God has done for us. In some circles it would be described as a "wholeheartedness talk." It might be argued that this should come before the talk on being filled with the Spirit; that as we open all the doors of our house He fills each part with His Spirit. I am sure there is something in this, but the movement in Scripture is from Him to us. He blesses us out of sheer grace and mercy and we respond by giving ourselves to Him out of love. When we begin to understand and experience the love of God for us as we are filled with His Spirit, our only appropriate response is to give everything we have to Him.

At this stage we have a brief break and move around greeting one another and chatting briefly. By this time there is a lot to talk and laugh about and there is usually quite a din! After the break we sing a song of praise. We have an offering which covers the cost of those who could not afford to pay for all or part of the weekend. One of the exciting things about these weekends is that we almost always end up with exactly the amount in the offering to cover those we have subsidized. People are learning right from the start that in the Christian family those who have more should help those who have less.

I then explain the communion service (along the lines of *Questions of*

There is always a sense of great excitement and celebration.

Life, pages 228-229). This is a good opportunity to teach about the central service of the Christian faith. We then invite anyone who knows and loves Jesus Christ to receive Communion, should they wish, regardless of their denomination or background. We pass round the bread and drink, asking those who do not wish to receive it for some reason to pass it on to their neighbor. Many comment on the beautiful simplicity and unity in this, and some experience God's love for the first time as they relax and receive Communion.

After Communion is over, I invite people to stand and again ask the Holy Spirit to come and work among us. After waiting for a short time I ask members of the team to begin praying with those who would like prayer. At this stage it is important for each member of the team to have the courage and confidence to go and pray for those in their groups along the lines I have suggested earlier in this chapter. This prayer goes on for some time. I usually end the service with a song and the blessing at around 1:00 P.M., but prayer for some continues while the rest of us go to lunch.

After lunch we gather for five minutes to give thanks to our hosts and deal with any final administrative matters. We arrange to meet at the evening service (for those who are able to come), and reserve all the front seats of the church for those who have been on the weekend. For many it is their first time in the church. There is always a sense of great excitement and celebration on these occasions. The ministry of the Spirit continues and some are filled with the Spirit and receive gifts during or after the evening service.

HEALING EVENING

Another excellent opportunity for those on the course to learn about ministry is the healing evening (*Questions of Life*, chapter 13) which occurs during Week 9. The evening follows the normal pattern until after coffee. On this evening we do not then go into small groups: rather, we stay together for a practical healing session.

At this point we outline the model of healing prayer which we follow (*Questions of Life*, pages 212-214). We then explain that God sometimes gives words of knowledge (1 Cor. 12:8) which point out whom God wants us to pray for and which are also an aid to faith in this area. We have found that people receive these words in various ways. Some may get a mental picture of the part of the body which God wants to heal. Some will merely receive an impression, and others may sense that they hear or see words. We have found that one of the most common ways we receive words of knowledge is by what we call a "sympathy pain": someone senses pain in their body, which they know is not really theirs.

Simon Dixon, who has since become our organist, had a stabbing pain when he moved or when he was touched around his jaw or neck. It had been very painful for a year and a half, and he had been told it couldn't be cured. He had lots of medical tests, but the doctors did not know what was wrong. They thought it might be a brain tumor. He was finally diagnosed as having auricular neuralgia. He was on a lot of drugs and at times his vision was affected. A woman in our congregation called Emma had felt a pain in her jaw which she thought must be a sympathy pain and therefore a word of knowledge. As a result, after prayer for healing, he was sufficiently cured to come off the drugs and after further prayer was totally healed. Since then he has been perfectly healthy.

 We nearly always see conversions as well.

At the end of this explanation we ask if people sense that they have any words of knowledge. Usually there are many (often received by those who are relatively new Christians who have never had the disadvantage of being told that God does not speak to His people today). They expect God to speak to them and He does. We write down all the words of knowledge. Sometimes we go through the list one by one asking people to identify themselves (providing, of course, the condition described is not one likely to cause embarrassment). On other occasions we simply ask all those who want to respond to stand at the same time.

Next, we ask one of those who have responded (if they are willing) to be prayed for in public. We then get two or three experienced people to pray for the person to provide a model of how to pray for healing. Whoever is leading the evening explains exactly what is happening.

Then we arrange for two or three people to pray for each of those who have responded to the words of knowledge. We try to get those who have had the particular words of knowledge to pray for those who responded to them. By this time almost everyone on the course is involved in the ministry. If there are any people not involved, we suggest they join a group to watch and learn from what is going on.

It is very exciting to see those who have only recently come to Christ praying, often with great faith, for others in a similar position. We have seen some remarkable healings on these evenings and we nearly always see conversions as well. One teenager called Bill brought his mother, Judy, who was not a Christian, on an *Alpha Course*. She had enjoyed the course but was still quite skeptical about the healing evening. That night there was a word of knowledge for a shoulder injury. She responded and was healed. She said afterward, "Many things had happened to me during *Alpha* that were answers to prayer which I had tried to explain away as coincidences, but it was the healing that made me realize that I could no longer say it was a coincidence. I prayed in my heart and made a commitment." Since then she has been a helper on a number of *Alpha*

Courses, being increasingly involved in the organization and administration.

The ministry of the Spirit is crucial to *Alpha* —without it, it would not really be an *Alpha Course.* We have found that time and again God has honored simple requests for Him to send His Spirit among us. Amazing and profound changes always occur in people's lives as a result. We are continuing to see people give their lives to Christ, be filled with the Spirit, get excited about Jesus, and bring their friends to the next course.

Notes

CHAPTER 1: HISTORY

1. As quoted in *Alpha News*, "In Brief," November 1996, p. 33.
2. As quoted in *Alpha News*, "Conference Feedback," November 1996, p. 33.
3. As quoted in *Alpha News*, "The International Scene," November 1996, p. 26. Reprinted with permission from Holy Trinity Brompton, London. Originally quoted in *Christian Week*, a Canadian newspaper.
4. As quoted in *Alpha News*, "In Brief," November 1996, p. 33. Reprinted with permission from Holy Trinity Brompton, London. Originally printed in *The Prayer Book Society of Canada Newsletter* in July 1996.
5. Based on an article in *Alpha News*, "USA: One pastor's experience," February 1997, p. 26.

CHAPTER 2: PRINCIPLES

1. Statistics from 1992 Social Trends from the Central Statistical Office, London, England.
2. Leading missiologist David Bosch defines evangelism as the proclamation of salvation in Christ to those who do not believe in Him, calling them to repentance and conversion, announcing forgiveness of sin, inviting them to become living members of Christ's earthly community and to begin a life of service to others in the power of the Holy Spirit.
3. John Stott, *The Contemporary Christian* (Nottingham, England: IVP, 1992), p. 241.
4. Michael Green, *Evangelism through the Local Church* (London, England: Hodder & Stoughton, 1990), p. ix.
5. John Stott, *The Contemporary Christian* (Nottingham, England: InterVarsity Press, 1992), pp. 121, 127.
6. Graham Tomlin, *Evangelical Anglicans*, edited by R. T. France and A. E. McGrath (London:SPCK, 1993), pp. 82-95.
7. John Stott, *Issues Facing Christians Today* (London: Marshalls, 1984), p. xi.
8. For further reading on the kingdom of God, see Nicky Gumbel, *Questions of Life* (Colorado Springs: David C. Cook Publishing Co., 1996), pp. 201-204.
9. Wayne Grudem, *Systematic Theology* (Nottingham, England: IVP, 1994), pp. 763-787.
10. David Pawson, *Fourth Wave* (London, England: Hodder & Stoughton, 1993), pp. 36-37.
11. John Pollock, *John Wesley* (London, England: Hodder & Stoughton, 1989), p. 118.

12. George Whitefield's *Journal* (Edinburgh, Scotland: Banner of Truth, 1992).

13. Charles Finney, *Memoirs of Rev. Charles G. Finney* (New York: Fleming H. Revell, 1876), p. 19.

14. John Pollock, *Moody without Sankey* (London, England: Hodder & Stoughton, 1963), pp. 83, 87.

15. Ibid, p.83.

16. R. A. Torrey, *The Baptism with the Holy Spirit* (Denville, NJ: Dimension Books, 1972), pp. 11, 54.

17. John Pollock, *Billy Graham* (London, England: Hodder & Stoughton, 1966), pp. 62-63.

CHAPTER 3: PRACTICALITIES

1. Nicky Gumbel, *Questions of Life* (Colorado Springs, CO: David C. Cook Publishing Co., 1996).

2. Nicky Gumbel, *Why Jesus?* (Colorado Springs, CO: David C. Cook Publishing Co., 1996).

3. Nicky Gumbel, *Why Christmas?* (Colorado Springs, CO: David C. Cook Publishing Co., 1996).

4. The information about daytime *Alpha* was originally developed by Deidre Hurst. She has run daytime *Alpha* at Holy Trinity Brompton Church in London for many years as well as leading *Alpha Courses* in other parts of England.

CHAPTER 4: GIVING TALKS

1. *Church Times*, September 7, 1989.

2. C. H. Spurgeon, *Lectures to My Students* (London, England: Marshall Pickering, 1954), p. 77.

3. Phillips Brooks, *Lectures on Preaching: The Yale Lectures* (Dutton, 1877; Allenson, 1895; Baker, 1969), p. 28.

CHAPTER 5: LEADING SMALL GROUPS

1. Nicky Gumbel, *Searching Issues* (Colorado Springs, CO: David C. Cook Publishing Co., 1996).

CHAPTER 6: PASTORAL CARE

1. Juan Carlos Ortiz, quoted in *Alpha* Magazine (Surrey, England: Trinity Square Publishing Ltd., January 1993).

2. R. A. Torrey, *Personal Work* (London, England: Pickering & Inglis, 1974), pp. 9-10.

CHAPTER 7: MINISTRY

1. *The New Bible Dictionary* (Nottingham: InterVarsity Press, 1962), p. 827.

Part III

Resources

Alpha Course Job Descriptions

This Appendix includes job descriptions for the positions listed below. Note that positions vary by size of the *Alpha Course* as suggested on pages 54-55. Small courses are defined as 1 or 2 small groups (or up to 25 people); medium courses as 3 to 9 small groups (or 25 to 120 people); and large courses as 10 or more small groups (or more than 120 people).

These job descriptions are included to help you organize your *Alpha Course*. Do not feel that you need to structure exactly as suggested. Adapt the job descriptions as needed to fit the size of your course and the talents of your team.

Alpha Leader (all courses regardless of size)

Director (all courses regardless of size)

Alpha Team

    Small-Group Coordinator (larger medium and large courses)

        Small-Group Leaders

        Small-Group Helpers

    Task Force Coordinator (larger medium and large courses)

        Alpha Dinner Coordinator (larger medium and large courses)

        Task Force Members (medium and large courses)

        Book Table Coordinator (larger medium and large courses)

    Treasurer

    Worship Leader (all but the smallest courses)

    Weekend Retreat Coordinator

        Alpha Weekend Entertainment Coordinator

Alpha Leader

The *Alpha* Leader is responsible for the spiritual leadership for the entire *Alpha* ministry. Spiritual leadership is provided for the Director, all members of the *Alpha* Team (all course coordinators, Small-Group Leaders and Helpers, and Worship and Task Force Members), and the guests.

QUALIFICATIONS

A spiritually mature Christian who has a heart for the lost; understands and agrees with the philosophy and theology of the *Alpha* ministry; understands the work of the Holy Spirit; is "full of the Spirit and wisdom" (Acts 6:3); is good with people; and is gifted in the areas of leadership, teaching, discernment, healing, or faith.

SPECIFIC RESPONSIBILITIES

1. Provide spiritual leadership for all aspects of the *Alpha* ministry including team training, weekly sessions, ministry times, and the weekend retreat.

2. Provide guidance for all practical aspects of the *Alpha* ministry as needed.

3. Determine with the church staff and *Alpha* Team whether the talks will be presented live or via audio- or videotape. If live, determine who will give each talk. (The *Alpha* Leader will usually present the majority of the talks.)

4. In conjunction with the Small-Group Coordinator, select all Small-Group Leaders and Small-Group Helpers.

5. Be sensitive to the spiritual and emotional needs of the *Alpha* Team and *Alpha* guests. Offer pastoral care as needed.

6. Prepare for each worship time by praying for the speaker (if someone other than yourself), the *Alpha* Worship Leader, the *Alpha* Team Members, the guests, and yourself. Ask the Holy Spirit to reveal any area of your life where you need forgiveness and to fill you.

7. Be familiar with the philosophy of pastoral care and ministry during *Alpha*. Principles and methods of pastoral care are included in chapter 6 of *How to Run the Alpha Course*, Tape 3 of *The Alpha Conference Tapes*, and Session 2 of *The Alpha Leader's Training Tapes* or *Videos*. Ministry during *Alpha* is covered in chapter 7 of *How to Run the Alpha Course*, Tape 5 of *The Alpha Conference Tapes*, and Session 3 of *The Alpha Leader's Training Tapes* or *Videos*.

8. Impart these principles and vision of the *Alpha* Ministry to the *Alpha* Team through three training sessions. The first two sessions (Leading Small Groups and Pastoral Care) will be held during the two weeks immediately preceding the course. The third session (Ministry during *Alpha*) will be held one week prior to the weekend retreat.

9. During the ministry times, pray for those who respond and indicate they would like prayer. Ministry times are included during the weekend retreat and following the talk "Does God Heal Today?" Remember the guidelines to pray in teams with a designated leader and to pray for members of your same sex.

10. Model spiritual leadership by being available to all team members, praying for them regularly, and consistently affirming them.

11. Represent the *Alpha* ministry in all church committee and board meetings.

Director (or Administrator)

The Director is responsible—with the help of the *Alpha* Team and *Alpha* Task Force—for all the practical aspects of setting up and running an *Alpha Course* including all phases of *Alpha* (the *Alpha* Dinner, the 10 weekly sessions, the *Alpha* Weekend, and the Celebration Dinner). The Director's amount of involvement with the specific details of *Alpha* will vary by the size of the course. In smaller courses the Director will have more hands-on involvement, and as a course grows, this person will delegate more to an *Alpha* leadership team as detailed in the suggested following job descriptions.

QUALIFICATIONS

A spiritually mature Christian who has a heart for the lost; understands and agrees with the philosophy and theology of the *Alpha* ministry; sees *Alpha* as an ongoing ministry, not a onetime event; and possesses gifts in the area of leadership, administration, and helps.

SPECIFIC RESPONSIBILITIES

1. Oversee the planning and running of the *Alpha Course*.

2. Assist the *Alpha* Leader in selecting an *Alpha* Team as needed depending on course size.

3. Schedule monthly planning and prayer meetings with all coordinators and team leaders. Report progress to the *Alpha* Leader.

4. Work with the *Alpha* Leader to provide team members with training, clear instructions, and deadlines for their areas of responsibility.

5. Encourage team members to prepare for the ministry times and each session with prayer.

6. During the course conduct weekly administration and prayer meeting. For larger courses, this responsibility can be delegated to the Small-Group Coordinator.

7. Model spiritual leadership by being available to all team members, praying for them regularly, and consistently affirming them.

8. With the Book Table Coordinator, determine quantity of all course materials (*The Alpha Course Manual* and *Leader's Guide, Why Jesus?* or *Why Christmas? Questions of Life,* and *How to Run the Alpha Course*) and related reading (see complete listing on pages 151-152).

9. Order and maintain an adequate quantity of *Alpha* resources and related reading. (See page 154 for ordering information.) In larger courses, oversee the Book Table Coordinator who will order and maintain resources for the book table.

10. If using *The Alpha Course Videos,* make sure videos 3, 4, and 5 are available at the Weekend Retreat.

11. Conduct an evaluation of the ministry with the help of the *Alpha* Team and the "*Alpha* Questionnaire" (see page 145).

12. Schedule a post *Alpha* evaluation meeting. Based on the completed questionnaires, determine necessary changes and adjustments to increase the effectiveness of the *Alpha* ministry.

APPENDIX A: JOB DESCRIPTIONS

The Small-Group Coordinator

Serves as a member of the Alpha *Team and reports to the Director.*

The key responsibility of this person is to recruit, oversee, and encourage Small-Group Leaders and Helpers.

QUALIFICATIONS

Experienced in facilitating small-group interaction; organized; able to encourage others; understands that the purpose of the small groups during *Alpha* is to provide a safe place for non-Christians to interact and respond to the talks; has good interpersonal skills; sensitive; gifted in areas of hospitality and evangelism; and has a servant's heart.

SPECIFIC RESPONSIBILITIES

1. With the *Alpha* Leader and Director, select Small-Group Leaders and Helpers. When recruiting leaders, ask, "If I had a non-churchgoing friend for whom I had been praying for years, would I be totally confident about putting him or her in _____'s group?"

2. Attend all training sessions, the opening *Alpha* Dinner, all weekly administrative/prayer meetings, each of 10 weekly *Alpha* sessions, the weekend retreat, any follow-up meetings, and the Celebration Dinner.

3. Model spiritual leadership by being available to all Small-Group Leaders and Helpers, praying for them regularly, and affirming them consistently.

4. Remind leaders and helpers that they do not have to "teach"; rather, they are to create a welcoming atmosphere where guests feel free to ask honest questions about the Christian faith.

5. With the *Alpha* Director, assign all leaders, helpers, and guests to small groups.

6. Make sure each group has enough copies of *The Alpha Course Manual*.

7. Encourage leaders and helpers to begin praying for their group members as soon as assignments are made and daily thereafter.

8. Emphasize to all leaders and helpers the importance of commitment to the course.

The Small-Group Leaders

Serve as part of the Ministry Team and report to the Small-Group Coordinator.

The key responsibility of the Small-Group Leader is to facilitate discussion in the small groups and to create a welcoming atmosphere where guests feel free to ask honest questions about the Christian faith.

QUALIFICATIONS

A growing Christian; has at least the beginnings of the gift of evangelism; is good with people; sensitive; understands the work of the Holy Spirit; is "full of the Spirit and wisdom" (Acts 6:3); understands from where nonchurchgoers or non-Christians are coming; nonjudgmental; and has a servant's heart.

SPECIFIC RESPONSIBILITIES

1. Attend all training sessions, the opening *Alpha* Dinner, all weekly administrative/ prayer meetings, each of 10 weekly *Alpha* sessions, the weekend retreat, any follow-up meetings, and the Celebration Dinner.

2. Read *Questions of Life* and *Searching Issues* (both by Nicky Gumbel) prior to *Alpha* to become familiar with the course content and objections to the Christian faith which may arise during the course.

3. Prepare for each small-group time by reviewing the material and praying for the speaker, the other leaders and helpers, and each group member. Be prepared to lead a Bible study when your group is ready and as outlined in *The Alpha Course Leader's Guide*.

4. Be familiar with the material in chapter 5 of *How to Run the Alpha Course* and pages 18–44 of *The Alpha Course Leader's Guide*. If at all possible do not have the Leader's Guide in plain view during group time, especially during the early sessions. You want group members to discuss freely and not to feel you are following a script.

5. Be sensitive to the spiritual and emotional needs of all *Alpha* participants. Offer pastoral care as needed.

6. Prepare for each worship time by praying for the speaker, the Worship Leader, other Worship and Ministry Team Members, the guests, and yourself. Ask the Holy Spirit to reveal any area of your life where you need forgiveness and to fill you.

7. During the ministry times, pray for those who respond and indicate they would like prayer. Ministry times follow Talks 9 and 12. Remember the guidelines to pray in teams with a designated leader and to pray for members of your same sex.

REMINDERS FOR LEADING EFFECTIVE SMALL GROUPS

1. Become a facilitator (simply another member of the group who is helping to make the discussion happen). Seek to guide and steer the group to truth rather than dictate terms or sit in judgment.

2. Look for opinions, not answers. Ask what the person thinks or feels.

3. Foster an environment of open discussion. The participants will feel like it is their group and will be more likely to own what they discover and learn.

4. Pray for each person before, during, and after each group time. Prayer is your most important task.

5. Communicate clearly in what ways you need your helpers to assist.

The Small-Group Helpers

Serve as part of the Ministry Team and report to the Small-Group Leader.

The key responsibility of the Small-Group Helpers is to assist the Small-Group Leaders create a welcoming atmosphere where guests feel free to ask honest questions about the Christian faith.

QUALIFICATIONS

A growing Christian or seeking non-Christian; is good with people; sensitive; understands from where nonchurchgoers are coming; nonjudgmental; and has a servant's heart.

SPECIFIC RESPONSIBILITIES

1. Attend all training sessions, the opening *Alpha* Dinner, all weekly administrative/ prayer meetings, each of 10 weekly *Alpha* sessions, the weekend retreat, any follow-up meetings, and the Celebration Dinner.

2. Read *Questions of Life* and *Searching Issues* (both by Nicky Gumbel) prior to the beginning of *Alpha* to become familiar with the course content and objections to the Christian faith which may come up during the course.

3. Prepare for each small-group time by reviewing the material and praying for the speaker, the other leaders and helpers, and each group member.

4. Be familiar with the material in chapter 5 of *How to Run the Alpha Course* and pages 18–44 of *The Alpha Course Leader's Guide*. If at all possible do not have the Leader's Guide in plain view during group time, especially during the early sessions. You want group members to discuss freely and not to feel you are following a script.

5. Help the discussion stay on course by asking questions.

6. Pray for each person before, during, and after every group time. Prayer is your most important task.

7. Assist your leaders in any way you are asked.

8. Prepare for each worship time by praying for the speaker, the *Alpha* Worship Leader, other Worship and Ministry Team Members, the guests, and yourself. Ask the Holy Spirit to reveal any area of your life where you need forgiveness and to fill you.

9. During the ministry times, pray for those who respond and indicate they would like prayer. Ministry times follow Talks 8 and 12. Remember the guidelines to pray in teams with a designated leader and to pray for members of your same sex.

10. If needed during the first three weeks, serve as a Greeter or Runner. See pages 118-119 for job descriptions.

The Greeters

Serve as members of the Alpha *Team and report to the Small-Group Coordinator.*

The Greeters are very important because they are among the first people the guests will meet. Their key responsibility is to make people feel welcome and glad they have come to *Alpha*.

QUALIFICATIONS
Friendly (without being effusive); helpful; easygoing; good at remembering names and faces; reliable; nice outward appearance; and have a servant's heart.

SPECIFIC RESPONSIBILITIES

1. Be familiar with each small group and that group's leaders, helpers, and members.

2. Know the location of each small group.

3. Inform each person of his or her small-group leader and location.

4. Assign guests who have not preregistered to an appropriate small group.

5. Introduce guests to a Runner who will take them to their small groups.

APPENDIX A: JOB DESCRIPTIONS

The Runners

Serve as members of the Alpha *Team and report to the Small-Group Coordinator.*

Since Runners are among the first people the guests meet, they are very important. Their main responsibility is to help people who are unfamiliar with the church and *Alpha* feel comfortable.

QUALIFICATIONS

Friendly (without being effusive); helpful; good at remembering names and faces; reliable; nice outward appearance; and have a servant's heart.

SPECIFIC RESPONSIBILITIES

1. Be familiar with each small group and that group's leaders, helpers, and members.

2. Display name tags for all team members and guests alphabetically and distribute them as people arrive.

3. Greet each guest as he or she is introduced by a Greeter and get that person to the correct small group.

4. Make name tags for guests who have not preregistered.

5. Return to the main door as quickly as possible after showing a guest to his or her group.

The Task Force Coordinator

Serves as a member of the Alpha *Team and reports to the Director.*

The key responsibility of this person is to select and train the *Alpha* Task Force—a team of people who provide practical services for the *Alpha Course* involving everything from helping with parking cars to cleanup.

QUALIFICATIONS

A mature or growing Christian; experienced in overseeing and delegating responsibility to others; organized; able to train others; understands that the heart of *Alpha* is to provide a safe and comfortable environment where nonchurchgoers feel welcome; has good interpersonal skills; sensitive; gifted in areas of administration and help; and has a servant's heart.

SPECIFIC RESPONSIBILITIES

1. Under the direction of the *Alpha* Leader and Director select and oversee the Task Force—a team of people who are responsible for logistics for the 10 weekly sessions, the *Alpha* Dinner (whether it is the first one before the first course begins or one after a course ends), and, in some cases, the Weekend Retreat. The size of the Task Force will vary depending on the number of people in attendance. Larger courses may want to appoint a person as the *Alpha* Dinner Coordinator (a separate job description is included). For smaller courses, the Task Force Coordinator can assume this responsibility.

2. Plan for all aspects of the weekly dinners including the menu, arrangement of tables, serving and eating dishes, cups and silverware, logistics of serving, cleanup, and evaluation.

3. Model spiritual leadership by being available to Task Force Members, praying for them regularly, and consistently affirming them.

4. Provide pastoral care as needed.

5. Attend all training sessions, the opening *Alpha* Dinner, all weekly administrative/ prayer meetings, each of 10 weekly *Alpha* sessions, the Weekend Retreat, any follow-up meetings, and the Celebration Dinner.

6. Oversee the setup and location for each small group, assuring adequate lighting, temperature control, and seating. Make sure there are enough copies of a modern translation of the Bible, such as the New International Version, for each Small-Group Leader, Helper, and member to use during group time.

7. Emphasize to all Task Force Members the importance of commitment to the course. Remind them that they want to try for a standard of "100 percent excellence."

8. Lead (or delegate leadership for) a prayer time with the Task Force Members during the small-group meeting time.

9. Perform all the above functions as needed at the weekend retreat under the direction of the Weekend Retreat Coordinator. If the retreat is held at a full-service conference center, the Task Force will simply attend the retreat. It becomes their chance to relax and worship.

APPENDIX A: JOB DESCRIPTIONS

The Alpha Dinner Coordinator

Serves as a member of the Task Force and reports to the Task Force Coordinator.

The key responsibility of this person is to assure that enough quality food is prepared and available for the opening *Alpha* Dinner, each weekly dinner, and the Celebration Dinner at the end of the course.

QUALIFICATIONS

A growing Christian; organized; is good with people; "full of the Spirit and wisdom" (Acts 6:4); has gifts in the areas of helps and administration; and has a servant's heart.

SPECIFIC RESPONSIBILITIES

If the weekly meals are not catered:

1. In conjunction with the Task Force Coordinator, plan a menu for each weekly dinner. These dinners should be simple yet appetizing. Suggestions include pasta dishes (spaghetti, lasagna, mostaccioli, etc.), sloppy joe's or barbecues, chili con carne, one-dish casseroles, and pizza. Always have a vegetarian alternative. In addition to the main dish serve a vegetable or gelatin salad, bread or rolls, and a simple dessert.

2. Based on the size of the course, determine who will cook. With groups of 12-15, the leaders and helpers can take turns. For courses with up to about 10 groups (or 120 people), the small groups can take turns with the cooking. Once the attendance goes over 120-150 it works best to have a caterer. Try to keep the cost of the dinner to $2.50 to $3.00 per person.

If the weekly meals are catered:

1. In conjunction with the Treasurer and the caterer, determine the weekly menu to provide a variety of inexpensive meals. Check with fast food and other local restaurants as many offer catering. Try to keep the weekly cost below $5.00 per person.

2. Agree with the caterer on the number of servings needed. This may vary for the first few weekly dinners depending on how many guests continue coming.

OPENING ALPHA DINNER, CLOSING CELEBRATION DINNER

1. Select a menu that is similar to, but a little nicer than, the weekly dinners. Think in terms of what could be served for company rather than for family. If possible, cater this meal.

2. Communicate the actual cost to the Task Force Coordinator who will make sure all Small-Group Leaders tell the members of their groups. Group members pay for their own meals and their guests.

WEEKEND RETREAT

1. In conjunction with the Weekend Retreat Coordinator, determine what meals or snacks, if any, will be brought or prepared by the church.

2. Oversee the purchase and preparation of any food brought in for the weekend.

Task Force Members

> *Serve as members of the Task Force and report to the Task Force Coordinator.*

The Task Force is to provide practical services for all aspects of the *Alpha* Course.

QUALIFICATIONS

A growing Christian; is good with people; moving toward being "full of the Spirit and wisdom" (Acts 6:4); has beginning of gifts in the areas of helps and mercy; and has a servant's heart.

SPECIFIC RESPONSIBILITIES

1. Help with parking cars—an important job. Remember that at the beginning of the course, those parking cars are the first people the guests will meet. Make sure to wear a smile and your name tag all the time to help guests feel welcome and get acquainted quickly.

2. Help serve the meal (unless done by the caterer) and make sure the guests have everything they need.

3. Set up all tables needed for the serving of dinner and coffee and all chairs for the small groups. Ensure that each small group is identified with a sign naming the group leaders and that each group has enough chairs, Bibles, and *Alpha Course Manuals.*

4. Place a pile of Bibles under one of the chairs in each small group. In this way the guests are not put off by seeing a Bible on every chair.

5. Prepare coffee, water for tea, and anything else needed for the coffee break.

6. If there is a book table with *Alpha* resources and related recommended books, help staff this table as needed.

7. Clean up tables, the serving area, and kitchen after the weekly dinners and Celebration Dinner.

8. Be willing to help in any way needed or as requested by the Task Force Coordinator.

APPENDIX A: JOB DESCRIPTIONS

The Book Table Coordinator

Serves as a member of the Alpha *Team and reports to the Task Force Coordinator.*

The key responsibility of this person is to order and maintain a stock of *Alpha* resources and related reading.

QUALIFICATIONS

A mature or growing Christian; experienced in overseeing and delegating responsibility to others; organized; has good interpersonal skills; gifted in areas of administration and help; and has a servant's heart.

SPECIFIC RESPONSIBILITIES

1. With the *Alpha* Director, determine quantity of all course materials *(The Alpha Course Manual* and *Leader's Guide, Why Jesus?* or *Why Christmas? Questions of Life, The Alpha Course* Videos or Tapes, *Searching Issues, How to Run the Alpha Course,* etc.) and related reading (see complete listing 151-157).

2. Order and maintain an adequate quantity of *Alpha* resources and related reading. (See page 154 for ordering information.)

The Treasurer

Serves as a member of the Alpha *Team and reports to the Director.*

This person is responsible for handling all budgets and finances related to the *Alpha Course.*

QUALIFICATIONS

Experienced accountant or treasurer; reliable; honest; prompt; and has a servant's heart.

SPECIFIC RESPONSIBILITIES

1. Prepare a budget for all aspects of the *Alpha* ministry including *Alpha* resources, cost of all meals and related expenses (flowers for Celebration Dinner, copy of *Why Jesus?* or *Why Christmas?* for each guest, caterer, etc.). See pages 52-54 for more information.

2. Meet with church treasurer/business manager to learn about church policies and procedures pertaining to the handling of funds.

3. In conjunction with the *Alpha* Dinner Coordinator, determine the cost of each weekly dinner. Collect money each week by placing baskets on each serving table.

4. Issue payment to the outside caterer or reimburse the *Alpha* Dinner Coordinator or whoever paid for the dinner supplies.

5. In conjunction with the *Alpha* Dinner Coordinator and the caterer, determine the per person cost for the Celebration Dinner and make this amount known to all *Alpha Course* participants by Week 8. People will pay for their own meal as well as the meals of any guests. All payments should be collected prior to the actual night of the dinner.

6. In conjunction with the Weekend Retreat Coordinator determine the per person cost of the weekend retreat. Publicize and collect funds at the time of registration.

7. Assist as needed in raising scholarships for those needing help to attend the event. This may be done with a collection on Sunday morning of the retreat.

8. Arrange for a lockbox, if needed, at the weekend retreat site to secure funds received on-site.

9. Develop a system of accountability for all income and expense associated with *Alpha.* (How is cash handled? Do checks need two signatures? How is registration income for the weekly dinner and weekend retreat accounted for? What safeguards are in place to insure integrity with all funds?)

10. Check on insurance coverage. Does your church have a policy that already covers any church-sponsored events? What insurance coverage is required by the weekend retreat facility, if any? Make sure the weekend retreat is adequately covered.

11. At the end of each retreat and each *Alpha Course,* produce an income and expense report for the *Alpha* Director and church treasurer.

APPENDIX A: JOB DESCRIPTIONS

The Worship Leader

Serves as a member of the Alpha *Team and reports to the Director.*

This person oversees all aspects of worship times during the weekly *Alpha* sessions and the weekend retreat.

QUALIFICATIONS

Competent musician and song leader; responsible; has understanding of philosophy of worship during *Alpha*; is versatile with music that appeals both to unchurched and growing Christian; has positive, teachable attitude; demonstrates mature Christian character; and has a servant's heart.

SPECIFIC RESPONSIBILITIES

1. In conjunction with the Director, select songs for each worship time during *Alpha* including weekly sessions and the weekend retreat. Plan to use a mixture of old and new songs, beginning with a familiar hymn the first night and moving toward more modern songs. Change gradually from singing about God to singing directly to God.

2. Select a team of musicians whose lives well represent the Christian faith.

3. In conjunction with the Director, arrange for all sound equipment needed for the worship times and presentation and taping of the talks (if given live).

4. Arrange for songbooks or overheads with the words to all songs to be used during the weekly sessions and weekend away. Make sure use of all music and words of songs comply with copyright laws. If your church is a member of CCLI, please be sure to report this copying activity on your CCLI survey.

5. If the talks are presented via videotape, make arrangements for the video player and enough monitors (or a screen large enough) that everyone present will be able to view it easily.

6. If the talks are presented live, make sure that the microphone is in place and working properly, there is a podium or music stand for the speaker to place notes, and water is available for the speaker.

7. Attend all training sessions, the opening *Alpha* Dinner, all weekly administrative/prayer meetings, each of 10 weekly *Alpha* sessions, the weekend retreat, any follow-up meetings, and the Celebration Dinner.

The Weekend Retreat Coordinator

Serves as a member of the Alpha *Team and reports to the Director.*

The key responsibility of this person is to plan and oversee the Weekend Retreat (or weekend away) by selecting and directing a team of workers who will facilitate all the practical aspects of the weekend.

QUALIFICATIONS

A mature or growing Christian; experienced in overseeing and delegating responsibility to others; organized; able to train others; understands that the heart of *Alpha* is to provide a safe and comfortable environment where nonchurchgoers feel welcome; has good interpersonal skills; sensitive; gifted in areas of administration and help; and has a servant's heart.

SPECIFIC RESPONSIBILITIES

1. Select and oversee people to organize the following aspects of the Weekend Retreat:

   • One-on-one informal counseling

   • Saturday evening entertainment

   • Sports and other free-time activities on Saturday afternoon

   • Child care, if you decide to have children come with their parents

   • Sunday morning Communion

2. Select and confirm a location for the weekend away within a one- or two-hour drive. During site selection ask the following questions:[1]

   • Can you handle a group of _____ (numbers) people on _____ (dates)? What is the maximum and minimum number of registrants your facility can accommodate?

   • What room accommodations are available? Can you provide sleeping rooms for the number of people expected? Are bathrooms private?

   • What is the size of your largest meeting room? What is the cost?

   • What food services can you provide and at what cost? (Obtain prices for snacks and meals; find out if the gratuity is included.) May we bring our own food, beverages, and/or snacks?

   • What meeting room equipment is provided (sound system, podium, overhead projector, etc.)? Will using this equipment cost extra? May we bring our own equipment?

   • What recreational facilities do you have? When are they open?

3. Obtain an agreement in writing from the facility specifying everything you discussed—menu, all costs for rooms and food, tips, meeting rooms, payment due dates and method, room types and prices, food or equipment you may bring, etc. Keep a copy on file at the church and carry a copy with you to the facility.

4. Obtain a map of how to get to the facility and a diagram of the facility. Duplicate and distribute this information to all attending.

5. Two or three weeks before the retreat, distribute a copy of the *"Alpha* Weekend Sign-Up Form" to each Small-Group Leader. A reproducible copy of this form is on page 148. This form serves two purposes:

APPENDIX A: JOB DESCRIPTIONS

- To obtain information from those who will attend regarding special diets, need for rides, requests to room together, etc.

- To provide information to those planning to attend regarding cost and location.

Also provide a copy of the weekend schedule, map to the facility, and list of what to bring for each small-group member.

6. Check with the responsible person that the following items are available at the retreat site:

- Task Force Leader—Books from the recommended reading list; supplies for Sunday morning Communion and for snacks and meals as planned.

- Worship Leader— Any audio/video equipment needed; songbooks or overhead transparencies.

- Treasurer—Cash box; checks to pay for all expenses; calculator; baskets for Sunday morning offering (which will be used to offset any amount individuals cannot afford); and all registration information including how much each person has paid.

- *Alpha* Dinner Coordinator—Food and beverage for any snacks or meals prepared and brought in by the church.

7. Make room assignments based on information obtained on the Weekend Sign-Up Form. Have this information available as people arrive.

[1]This information has been adapted from *Creative Weekends*, compiled by Paul Petersen (Colorado Springs: David C. Cook Publishing Co., 1995), p. 234. Used with permission.

The Weekend Entertainment Coordinator

Serves as part of the Alpha *Team and reports to the Weekend Retreat Coordinator.*

This person is responsible for organizing and directing the Saturday evening entertainment during the weekend retreat.

QUALIFICATIONS

A mature or growing Christian; experienced in overseeing others; organized; has a good sense of humor; works well with people; has a servant's heart.

SPECIFIC RESPONSIBILITIES

1. Publicize the Saturday entertainment night beginning one or two weeks prior to the weekend retreat.

2. Set up times for individuals or groups to register their "acts." Obtain the following information for each potential act: names, phone numbers, the type of act, content or script, and approximate length.

3. Screen all entertainment, making sure it is wholesome and inoffensive to Christians and non-Christians alike. The intent of this evening is good, clean fun. Therefore, avoid anything "religious" and don't expect professional quality. Everything from skits, stand-up comedy, and singing, to "magic," monologues, and dramatic readings work well.

4. Develop a sequence for the Saturday night program which offers variety. That is, you do not want three soloists in a row!

5. Serve as emcee for the talent review.

6. Lead the audience in affirming each person who is brave enough to participate in the entertainment.

APPENDIX A: JOB DESCRIPTIONS

Planning Timeline

Director_____ Phone (day) _____ (evening)_____

Date of *Alpha* Dinner _____ Date Course Starts _____

Thank you for agreeing to serve on the Alpha *Team or* Alpha *Task Force. Please check over this timeline for the tasks assigned to you. Adapt as needed. Supplement this timeline with your specific job description. Highlight your tasks and due date each time they appear. Mark your calendar accordingly.*

7 TO 9 MONTHS IN ADVANCE
DATE _____

Alpha Leader

☐ Determine with the church staff and *Alpha* Team leaders whether the talks will be presented live or via tape. If any will be presented live, select the speaker(s) and assign the talks.

☐ Attend an *Alpha* Conference with the Director and as many of your *Alpha* Team leaders and church staff as possible.

Director

☐ Attend an *Alpha* Conference with as many of your *Alpha* Team leaders and church staff as possible.

☐ With the *Alpha* Leader set the exact dates for the opening *Alpha* Dinner, the *Alpha* Course, the weekend retreat, and the closing Celebration Dinner. Reserve all church facilities that will be needed for each event.

☐ Based on the anticipated size of the course, select a site for the *Alpha* Dinner and weekly meetings.

☐ With the *Alpha* Leader, select people to serve in the following roles: Small-Group Coordinator, Task Force Coordinator, Treasurer, Worship Leader, and Weekend Retreat Coordinator. Make sure each leader on the *Alpha* Team understands his or her responsibilities. Distribute copies of appropriate job descriptions to all *Alpha* Team members.

6 MONTHS IN ADVANCE
DATE _____

Director

☐ Hold the first *Alpha* Team meeting. Review this timeline, adjust as needed, and fill in due dates. Distribute a copy to each *Alpha* Team member.

☐ Seek God's guidance for the selection of Small-Group Leaders and Helpers.

Task Force Coordinator

☐ Based on the anticipated size of the course, determine whether you will need an *Alpha* Dinner Coordinator. Recruit this person if needed.

☐ In conjunction with the Treasurer, begin developing a budget for the *Alpha* Dinner (to be held before the beginning of your first *Alpha Course*), weekly *Alpha* sessions, Celebration Dinner (following each *Alpha* Course), and weekend retreat.

❏ Seek God's guidance in the selection of the *Alpha* Dinner Coordinator and other Task Force Members.

Treasurer

❏ Begin developing a budget for the course and the weekend retreat.

❏ Meet with the church treasurer/business manager to learn about church policies pertaining to handling funds. Throughout the *Alpha* ministry implement these policies.

Weekend Retreat Coordinator

❏ With the *Alpha* Team's input, carefully choose one or two facilities as potential locations for the weekend retreat. Contact and evaluate these facilities based on the anticipated retreat attendance and make a selection as soon as possible.

❏ Obtain a written agreement from the facility specifying everything you discussed.

❏ In conjunction with the Treasurer, develop a budget for the weekend retreat.

5 MONTHS IN ADVANCE
DATE _____

Director

❏ Meet with the *Alpha* Team to pray and discuss progress. Report progress to the *Alpha* Leader.

4 MONTHS IN ADVANCE
DATE _____

Director

❏ Meet with the *Alpha* Team to pray and discuss progress. Report progress to the *Alpha* Leader.

3 MONTHS IN ADVANCE
DATE _____

Director

❏ Meet with the *Alpha* Team to pray and discuss progress. Report progress to the *Alpha* Leader.

❏ Order (or make sure the Book Table Coordinator has ordered) an adequate supply of *Alpha* resources and any related reading. Make sure each member of the *Alpha* Team and Task Force has a copy of *Questions of Life* (the content of the *Alpha* Course in book form). All coordinators and Small-Group Leaders and Helpers should also read *How to Run the Alpha Course* and *Searching Issues* prior to the start of the course. Leaders and Helpers need copies of the *Alpha Course Manual* and *Leader's Guide*. Order enough copies of *Why Jesus?* (or *Why Christmas?* depending on the season) to distribute on the second *Alpha* Sunday and at the *Alpha* Dinner.

Small-Group Coordinator

❏ With the *Alpha* Leader and Director, select the Small-Group Leaders and Helpers. Determine which helpers will also serve on the Ministry Team.

❏ Send letter of invitation to serve (signed by the *Alpha* Leader) to all Small-Group Leaders and Helpers.

Task Force Coordinator

☐ Based on the size of your course, determine the size of the Task Force and select each member. Send letter of invitation to serve (signed by the *Alpha* Leader) to each Task Force Member.

☐ Meet with your team to assign jobs.

Treasurer

☐ Develop a system of accounting for all income and expenses for the course.

☐ Check on insurance coverage and make arrangements for coverage for all aspects of the course as needed.

Worship Leader

☐ Select a team of musicians and singers. Set a practice schedule to assure quality music each week and at the retreat.

☐ Arrange for all audio/video equipment for the weekly sessions and weekend.

2 MONTHS IN ADVANCE
DATE _____

Director

☐ Meet with the *Alpha* Team to discuss progress and pray for each team member and expected guest. Report progress to the *Alpha* Leader.

Small-Group Leaders/Helpers (Ministry Team)

☐ Read *Questions of Life* and *Searching Issues* and review *How to Run the Alpha Course* (Handbook) by Nicky Gumbel.

☐ Become familiar with the philosophy of pastoral care and ministry as explained in various *Alpha* resources. See job description.

4 WEEKS IN ADVANCE
DATE _____

Director

☐ Meet with the *Alpha* Team to discuss progress and pray for each team member and expected guest. Report progress to the *Alpha* Leader.

☐ Either customize the *Alpha* brochure (see pages 62-63 and 141 for more information) or create and print your own brochure. Write a brief letter of invitation which includes the dates, times, location, and phone of *Alpha* and the names of all the talks. (See page 147 for a sample letter.)

Task Force Coordinator or *Alpha* Dinner Coordinator

☐ Plan the weekly dinner menus.

☐ Make arrangements with the caterer or make cooking assignments.

Treasurer

☐ Finalize budget for all aspects of *Alpha* including each meal, the retreat, all flowers, resources, and other incidentals.

Worship Leader

☐ Select songs for each weekly session and the weekend retreat. As necessary, seek permission to print and display the words.

☐ Begin weekly practices to ensure quality music and singing at all *Alpha* events.

3 WEEKS IN ADVANCE
DATE _____

Director

❐ Meet with the Alpha Team to discuss progress and pray for each team member and expected guest. Report to *Alpha* Leader.

❐ Insert a flyer about *Alpha* in all worship bulletins. Have *Alpha* Registration brochures available at all services.

Weekend Retreat Coordinator

❐ Select people to organize and implement these aspects of the retreat: informal counseling, Saturday evening entertainment, free-time activities, child care, and the Sunday morning communion service.

2 WEEKS IN ADVANCE
DATE _____

Alpha Leader

❐ Meet with the *Alpha* Team to discuss progress and pray for each team member and expected guest.

❐ Conduct the first of three training sessions for the Small-Group Leaders and Helpers. The topic will be "Leading Small Groups."

Director

❐ Meet with the *Alpha* Team to discuss progress and pray for each team member and expected guest.

❐ Insert a flyer about *Alpha* in all worship bulletins. Have *Alpha* Registration brochures available at all services.

❐ Hold the first "*Alpha* Sunday." Share a true story of a life changed through attending *Alpha*. For your first *Alpha*, select one from *Alpha News* or *The God Who Changes Lives* by Mark Elsdon-Dew. For subsequent courses, plan on using impromptu interviews as explained on page 63. Encourage everyone to invite friends and family to church next Sunday.

Small-Group Coordinator

❐ With the Director, assign all leaders, helpers, and guests to small groups. Encourage the leaders and helpers to begin praying for their group members.

Small-Group Leaders/Helpers

❐ Attend the first of three training sessions. The topic will be "Leading Small Groups."

❐ Be familiar with the content of chapter 5 of *How to Run the Alpha Course* and pages 18-44 of the *Alpha Course Leader's Guide*.

Worship Leader

❐ Arrange for songbooks or overheads for all songs to be used throughout *Alpha*.

1 WEEK IN ADVANCE
DATE _____

Alpha Leader

❐ Hold the second of three training sessions. The topic will be "Pastoral Care."

Director

❐ Insert a flyer about *Alpha* in all worship bulletins. Have *Alpha* registration brochures available at all services.

☐ Hold the second *Alpha* Sunday. Include a short testimony of the impact of *Alpha*. Distribute brochures and complimentary copies of *Why Jesus?* (or *Why Christmas?* depending on the season) to anyone interested. The pastor's message should be evangelistic. Close the service with an invitation to attend *Alpha*.

Small-Group Leaders/Helpers (Ministry Team) and Task Force

☐ Attend the second of three training sessions. The topic will be "Pastoral Care."

Task Force Coordinator or *Alpha* Dinner Coordinator

☐ If using a caterer, make final arrangements for the number of expected guests.

ALPHA DINNER
DATE _____

Alpha Leader

☐ Present the talk "Christianity: Boring, Untrue, and Irrelevant?" or introduce the recorded talk.

Director

☐ Serve as the emcee. Keep the tone relaxed and friendly. Use of humor will help the guests relax.

Entire *Alpha* Team

☐ Arrive early with a servant's attitude. Pray for all aspects of the evening.

Alpha Dinner Coordinator

☐ Oversee all aspects of the preparation of the meal.

Task Force Coordinator

☐ Oversee all aspects of the serving and cleanup of the meal.

Task Force Members

☐ Welcome and serve the guests with natural friendliness.

☐ Set the tables and have copies of *Why Jesus?* (or *Why Christmas?*) at each door for guests to pick up on their way out.

☐ Make sure the room temperature is comfortable and the lighting is good.

☐ Complete all tasks as directed by the coordinator.

Worship Leader

☐ Make sure all audiovisual equipment is in place before guests arrive. If using video, set up the video player and monitor(s). For live speakers, make sure the microphone and podium are in place for the speaker.

WEEK 1 OF ALPHA
(and all other sessions during Alpha)
DATE _____

Alpha Leader

☐ Present the scheduled talk or introduce the recorded talk. See page 47 for sequence of talks.

☐ During the talks and ministry times, pray for each Ministry Team Member, and all who respond during the ministry times.

Director

☐ Conduct the administration and prayer meeting prior to each dinner.

Treasurer

❏ Place baskets on each serving table and collect money to cover the weekly dinners.

❏ Pay the outside caterer or reimburse those in the church who purchased the dinner supplies.

All *Alpha* Team Members

❏ Arrive in time for the weekly administration and prayer meeting.

Task Force Coordinator

❏ Oversee all practical aspects of the course.

❏ Lead (or delegate the leadership of) a prayer time with the Task Force Members while the small groups are meeting.

Task Force

❏ Set up chairs and display a sign for each small group. Make sure there are enough Bibles and *Alpha Course Manuals* for each group.

❏ Help park cars, greet guests, and direct them to their small groups. Make sure each guest and *Alpha* Team Member has a name tag.

❏ Serve food and beverages during the dinner and coffee break. Make sure the eating and meeting area(s) are spotless at the end of each session.

❏ Help with book sales at the book table.

Small-Group Leaders/Helpers (Ministry Team)

❏ Pray for the speaker, all other Small-Group Leaders and Helpers, the guests, and all aspects of *Alpha*.

Worship Leader

❏ Make sure all audiovisual equipment is in place before guests arrive. If using video, set up the video player and monitor(s). For live speakers, make sure the microphone and podium are in place after the worship time.

WEEK 2 OF ALPHA
DATE _____

Treasurer

❏ With the Weekend Retreat Coordinator, determine the cost per person for the retreat. Arrange for a lockbox at the weekend retreat.

Weekend Retreat Coordinator

❏ Distribute copies of the Alpha Weekend Sign-up Form to Small-Group Leaders. Include the weekend schedule, map to the facility, and list of what to bring.

WEEK 3 OF ALPHA
DATE _____

Weekend Entertainment Coordinator

❏ Begin publicizing the Saturday entertainment by providing sign-up sheets for individual or group "acts." Be sensitive to the feelings of the potential participants as you screen the "acts."

WEEK 4 OF ALPHA
DATE _____

Weekend Retreat Coordinator

❏ Finalize the count for the retreat. Make room assignments; have copies available at the registration table at the retreat.

☐ Meet with your team of volunteers to assure all aspects of the retreat are covered as listed in your job description.

WEEK 5 OF ALPHA
DATE _____

Task Force Coordinator or *Alpha* Dinner Coordinator
☐ Oversee the purchase and preparation of any food the church will provide at the weekend retreat.

Weekend Entertainment Coordinator
☐ Develop the order of entertainment and communicate this to each participant.

WEEK 6 OF ALPHA
DATE _____

Alpha Leader
☐ Present the talk "How Does God Guide Us?" or introduce the recorded talk.

WEEKEND RETREAT
DATE _____

☐ See job descriptions for specific information.

WEEK 7 OF ALPHA
DATE _____

Director
☐ Begin promoting the Celebration Dinner and distribute invitations for the small-group members to use with their friends and families.

Small-Group Leaders
☐ During the small-group time allow time for personal sharing about the weekend away.

WEEK 8 OF ALPHA
DATE _____

Task Force Coordinator or *Alpha* Dinner Coordinator
☐ Select a menu for the Celebration Dinner. Communicate the cost per dinner to the Task Force Coordinator who will give this information to the Small-Group Leaders.

Small-Group Leaders
☐ Distribute copies of the Celebration Dinner invitation to group members.

WEEK 9 OF ALPHA
DATE _____

Alpha Leader
☐ Oversee the Ministry Team during the ministry time.

Small-Group Leaders/Helpers (Ministry Team)
☐ Be available to pray for those who respond during the ministry time following the guidelines in chapter 7 of *How to Run the Alpha Course* and Session 3 of the *Alpha Leader's Training Tapes or Videos.*

WEEK 10 OF ALPHA
DATE _____

Treasurer

☐ Finalize the count for the Celebration Dinner. Collect payment for the Celebration Dinner for each person and his or her guests.

CELEBRATION DINNER
DATE _____

Alpha Leader

☐ Present the talk "Christianity: Boring, Untrue, and Irrelevant?" or introduce the recorded talk.

Director

☐ Serve as the emcee. Keep the tone relaxed and friendly. Use of humor will help the guests relax.

Entire *Alpha* Team

☐ Arrive early with a servant's attitude. Pray for all aspects of the evening.

Alpha Dinner Coordinator

☐ Oversee all aspects of the preparation of the meal.

Task Force Coordinator

☐ Oversee all aspects of the serving and cleanup of the meal.

Task Force Members

☐ Welcome and serve the guests with natural friendliness.

☐ Set the tables and have copies of *Why Jesus?* (or *Why Christmas?*) at each door for guests to pick up on their way out.

☐ Make sure the room temperature is comfortable and the lighting is good.

☐ Complete all tasks as directed by the coordinator.

Worship Leader

☐ Make sure all audiovisual equipment is in place before guests arrive. If using video, set up the video player and monitor(s). For live speakers, make sure the microphone and podium are in place for the speaker.

1 WEEK AFTER ALPHA COURSE ENDS
DATE _____

Director

☐ Meet with the *Alpha* Team to go over the completed *Alpha* Questionnaires, evaluate all aspects of the course, affirm and thank each person, and determine necessary changes for the next course. Make adjustments in the *Alpha* Team as needed to have all positions filled for the next course.

Small-Group Leaders

☐ Complete and turn in an *Alpha* Follow-up Form (see page 149 for a reproducible form).

Treasurer

☐ Prepare and submit an income and expense report for all *Alpha* expenses.

Schedules

SCHEDULE FOR EVENING ALPHA

5:15 or 5:30 P.M.	Leaders and helpers meet to pray
6:00 P.M.	Dinner is served
6:30 P.M.	Welcome
6:40 P.M.	Songs of worship
6:50 P.M.	Talk
7:45 P.M.	Coffee
8:00 P.M.	Small groups
9:00 P.M.	End

SCHEDULE FOR DAYTIME ALPHA

9:45 A.M.	Child care opens
10:05 A.M.	Welcome & coffee
	Worship
10:35 A.M.	Announcements
10:40 A.M.	Talk
11:20 A.M.	Small groups
12:00 P.M.	Child care ends

SCHEDULE FOR WEEKEND RETREAT

FULL WEEKEND SCHEDULE

Friday

5:30 P.M. onward	Arrive
7:00 P.M.	Dinner
9:15 P.M.	Worship and a brief introduction to the weekend

Saturday

8:00 A.M.	Breakfast
9:00 A.M.	Worship
	Talk 1 - "Who Is the Holy Spirit?"
10:15 A.M.	Coffee
10:45 A.M.	Talk 2 - "What Does the Holy Spirit Do?"
11:30 A.M.	Small group discussion
12:30 P.M.	Lunch
Free Afternoon	Optional sports and activities will be offered
3:30 P.M.	Optional refreshments
4:00 P.M.	Worship
	Talk 3 - "How Can I Be filled with the Spirit?"
6:00 P.M.	Dinner
8:00 P.M.	Talent Show (you are invited to participate)

Sunday

9:00 A.M.	Breakfast
9:45 A.M.	Small group discussion
10:30 A.M.	Worship
	Talk 4 - "How Can I Make the Most of the Rest of My Life?"
	Communion
1:00 P.M.	Lunch

Remember to bring:

- Bible, *Alpha Course Manual,* pen or pencil, and notebook
- Personal toiletries
- Sports gear (tennis racket, Frisbee, swimsuit, etc.)
- Props, costumes, music, or anything needed for the Talent Show!

ALL-DAY SATURDAY ONLY

8:00 A.M.	Arrive
8:30 A.M.	Worship
	Talk 1 - Combine "Who Is the Holy Spirit?" and "What Does the Holy Spirit Do?" (on Video 3, #8 and #9)
9:45 A.M.	Coffee
10:15 A.M.	Talk 2 - "How Can I Be Filled with the Holy Spirit? (on Video 4, #10)
Noon	Lunch
1:15 P.M.	Free afternoon
3:00 P.M.	Optional refreshments
4:00 P.M.	Worship
	Talk 3 - "How Can I Make the Most of the Rest of My Life?" (on Video 5, #15)
6:30 P.M.	Depart

WHAT OTHERS ARE SAYING ABOUT *ALPHA*

For as long as I can remember, through my childhood, teens, and adult years, I have asked questions. One question I constantly asked myself was "Do I believe in God?" I had no answer and it bothered me ... By the end of the third Alpha evening I had come to a few realizations that were truly stunning for me ... I knew that Jesus died for me and that I could never 'sit the fence' again. — JILL

I have learned more in the space of a few weeks than I ever had in years of attending church. — DAVID

Everything Alpha gave me was so positive; it gave me the beginnings of understanding what being a Christian means; it gave me warm friendship and a sense of belonging ... it gave me patient and thoughtful answers to all my questions. — SARAH

Alpha is wonderful—life changing! Alpha answered and clarified all the basics for me and put me on firm ground to travel forward on my journey with God. — MARY

From the very first meeting we felt this is what had been missing from our lives. It felt like coming home. — MARGARET AND KEITH

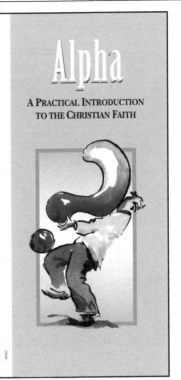

Alpha

A PRACTICAL INTRODUCTION TO THE CHRISTIAN FAITH

- What is the meaning of life?
- What happens when we die?
- What relevance does Jesus have for our lives?
- How do we deal with guilt?

If you would like to explore questions like these, then *Alpha* is for you.

WHAT IS *ALPHA*?

Alpha is for:

Anyone interested in finding out more about the Christian faith. Adults of all ages are welcome.

Learning and laughter. It is possible to learn about the Christian faith and to have fun at the same time.

People meeting together. An opportunity to get to know others and to make new friends.

Helping one another. The small groups give you a chance to discuss issues raised during the talks.

Ask anything. *Alpha* is a place where no question is seen as too simple or too hostile.

WHO IS *ALPHA* FOR?

Alpha is for everyone! It's especially geared to:

- People interested in investigating Christianity.
- Newcomers to the church.
- New Christians.
- Couples preparing for marriage.
- Christians who want to brush up on the basics.

WHAT HAPPENS AT *ALPHA*?

There is a series of talks on topics such as:

- Who Is Jesus?
- Why Did Jesus Die?
- Why and How Should I Read the Bible?
- Why and How Do I Pray?
- What About the Holy Spirit?
- How Can I Overcome Evil?
- Why and How Should I Tell Others?
- Does God Heal Today?
- What About the Church?

After each talk there is a small-group time for everyone to discuss any questions or issues they have. This gives an opportunity to get to know each other and to learn together.

WHEN AND WHERE?

The *Alpha* Course meets every week for ten weeks. See the back of this brochure for exact times and place.

We look forward to seeing you at:

Alpha

REGISTRATION FORM

Please fill in this form to let us know you are planning on coming.

NAME

ADDRESS

PHONE (DAY)

PHONE (EVE.)

It would be most helpful if you could give us an idea of your age.

If you would like to come to the next Alpha Course, please complete this form and return it to the address on the back.

The *Alpha* Registration Brochure (unfolded, front and back sides)
Note that you can customize the back panel to include the specific dates, times, and location of your local *Alpha Course*.

Press Release

THE ALPHA COURSE

(Name of sponsoring group/church) will begin *The Alpha Course* on (date), at (time), at (place).

This ten-week practical introduction to the Christian faith offers answers to some key questions. Each weekly session begins with an informal dinner, followed by a large-group learning time, and ends with small-group discussion and interaction. *Alpha* began in London and is now held in thousands of churches around the world. Join the thousands who have found answers to their questions about life and God and how they relate.

To learn more about the course, call (number of *Alpha* Director) or come to the *Alpha* Dinner on (date), at (time), at (location). For reservations, call (church number) between (daily hours).

Coming soon . . .

The Alpha Course

A 10-Week Practical Introduction to the Christian Faith

Anyone can come. Anyone interested in finding out more about the Christian faith is welcome.

Learning and laughter. Join others in a relaxed atmosphere.

Pasta (or other great food). Each weekly session begins with dinner.

Helping one another. Dinner is followed by large-group presentation and small-group discussion.

Ask anything. Here's your chance to ask your questions and express your opinions.

When:

Where:

For more information call:

PRESENTING

The Alpha Course

A 10-Week Practical Introduction to the Christian Faith

❖ Dinner ❖ Small-group discussion

❖ Group teaching ❖ Weekend retreat

A 10-week program for those who wonder:

❖ Christianity: Boring, Untrue, and Irrelevant?

❖ Who Is Jesus?

❖ Why Did Jesus Die?

❖ How Can I Be Sure of My Faith?

❖ Why and How Should I Read the Bible?

❖ Why and How Do I Pray?

❖ How Does God Guide Us?

❖ Who Is the Holy Spirit?

❖ How Can I Be Filled with the Spirit?

❖ What Does the Holy Spirit Do?

❖ How Can I Resist Evil?

❖ Why and How Should We Tell Others?

❖ Does God Heal Today?

❖ What About the Church?

Alpha Questionnaire

Name_____ Group _____

1. How did you hear about the *Alpha Course?*_____

   _____

2. Why did you decide to attend *Alpha?* _____

   _____

3. Did you attend the *Alpha* Dinner party?   ❑ yes   ❑ no

4. How many of the weekly sessions did you attend?_____

5. Did you attend the weekend retreat?   ❑ yes   ❑ no

6. Before you started the course, how would you have described yourself in terms of the Christian faith? _____

   _____

7. Were you a Christian when you started the course?   ❑ yes   ❑ no

8. Were you a churchgoer when you started the course?   ❑ yes   ❑ no

9. How would you describe yourself now in terms of the Christian faith? _____

   _____

If your answers to questions 6 and 9 are different, when and how did the change occur?

   _____

10. In what ways, if any, did you benefit from the *Alpha Course?* _____

    _____

11. What did you enjoy most about *Alpha?*_____

    _____

12. In what ways could the course be improved?

    Talks _____

    Small Groups _____

    Other_____

    anything
    else?

Sample Alpha Invitation Letter

Holy Trinity Brompton
Brompton Road, London SW7 1JA
Telephone: 0171 581 8255 Fax: 0171 589 3390

We would like to invite you to join us on the *Alpha Course* which begins Wednesday, January 19. Alpha is a short, practical introduction to the Christian faith. It includes an optional weekend away. This is a key part of the course, as well as being great fun, so please write the dates on your calendar now. Further details will be available later.

We will be leading the course with a team. Each evening begins with supper at 6:00 P.M., includes a talk, and ends with an opportunity to meet in small groups to discuss and study the Bible. All meetings will take place on Wednesday evenings at Holy Trinity Brompton.

Please return your complete registration form to the church office by January 6. We look forward to meeting you.

—Nicky and Pippa Gumbel

January 19	Who Is Jesus?
January 26	Why Did Jesus Die?
February 2	How Can I Be Sure of My Faith?
February 9	Why and How Should I Read the Bible?
February 16	Why and How Do I Pray?
February 23	How Does God Guide Us?
February 25-27	The Holy Spirit
	Weekend Retreat
March 1	How Can I Resist Evil?
March 8	Why and How Should We Tell Others?
March 15	Does God Heal Today?
March 22	What About the Church?
March 29	Alpha Dinner party (I)
April 5	Alpha Dinner party (II)

Alpha Weekend Sign-up Form

Group Number _____		Date _____	Amount Paid				Notes (Late arrivals, special diet, roommate requests, room in car, etc.)
First Name	Last Name		Total Due	Check	Cash	Amt. Due	

Alpha Follow-up Form

Alpha Date _____

Group Number _____

Please return your completed form by _____. Also let me know any ideas for improving the *Alpha Course*. Many thanks.

First Name	Last Name	Completed the course? Yes or No	If no, why not?	Record name of small group (if any)	*Alpha* helper? Task force? Testimony?

Suggested Reading & Alpha Resources

RELATED READING

The following books are recommended to complement the *Alpha Course*. While the suggested books follow the course sequence, they can be read in any order.

Talk 1 - Who Is Jesus?

Title	Author	Publisher	ISBN
Why Jesus?	Nicky Gumbel	Cook	0-7814-5260-0

Talk 2 - Why Did Jesus Die?

Title	Author	Publisher	ISBN
Questions of Life	Nicky Gumbel	Cook	0-7814-5261-9
Basic Christianity	John Stott	Intervarsity Press	0-87784-690-1
Mere Christianity	C. S. Lewis	Macmillan	0-02-086940-1
The Cross of Christ	John Stott	Intervarsity Press	0-87784-998-6

Talk 3 - How Can I Be Sure of My Faith?

Title	Author	Publisher	ISBN
The Cross and the Switchblade	David Wilkerson w/John & Elizabeth Sherrill	Baker Book House/ Revell	0-800-79070-7
The Hiding Place	Corrie Ten Boom	Barbour & Co., Inc.	0-916441-80-6
Born Again	Charles Colson	Baker Book House	0-91644-194-6

Talk 4 - Why and How Should I Read the Bible?

Title	Author	Publisher	ISBN
The NIV Study Bible		Zondervan Bible Publishers	0-310-90767-5
Unlocking the Bible	John Drane	Lion Publishing	0-7459-2210-4
Understanding the Bible	John Stott	Zondervan Publishing House	0-310-41431-8
What the Bible Is All About	Henrietta Mears	Gospel Light	0-8307-1390-5

Talk 5 - Why and How Do I Pray?

Title	Author	Publisher	ISBN
How to Pray	R. A. Torrey	Moody Press	0-8024-3709-5
Too Busy Not to Pray	Bill Hybels	Intervarsity Press	0-8308-1256-3
Don't Just Stand There, Pray Something	Ron Dunn	Thomas Nelson Publishers	0-8407-4393-9

Talk 6 - Who Is the Holy Spirit?

<u>Title</u>	<u>Author</u>	<u>Publisher</u>	<u>ISBN</u>
Chasing the Dragon	Jackie Pullinger	Servant Publications	089-283-151-0

Talk 7 - What Does the Holy Spirit Do?

<u>Title</u>	<u>Author</u>	<u>Publisher</u>	<u>ISBN</u>
The God Who Changes Lives	Mark Elsdon-Dew	Cook	0-7814-5272-4

Talk 8 - How Can I Be Filled with the Spirit?

Talk 9 - How Can I Resist Evil?

<u>Title</u>	<u>Author</u>	<u>Publisher</u>	<u>ISBN</u>
The Screwtape Letters	C. S. Lewis	Barbour & Co., Inc.	1-55748-240-3

Talk 10 - How Does God Guide Us?

Talk 11 - Why and How Should We Tell Others?

<u>Title</u>	<u>Author</u>	<u>Publisher</u>	<u>ISBN</u>
Searching Issues	Nicky Gumbel	Cook	0-7814-5259-7
Evidence That Demands a Verdict	Josh McDowell	Scripture Press	1-8720-5905-8
Know Why You Believe	Paul Little Marie Little	Victor Books	0-89693-080-7

Talk 12 - Does God Heal Today?

<u>Title</u>	<u>Author</u>	<u>Publisher</u>	<u>ISBN</u>
Power Healing	John Wimber Kevin Springer	HarperSanFran.	0-06-069533-1
Power Evangelism	John Wimber Kevin Springer	HarperSanFran.	0-06-069542-0

Talk 13 - What About the Church?

<u>Title</u>	<u>Author</u>	<u>Publisher</u>	<u>ISBN</u>
A Life Worth Living	Nicky Gumbel	Cook	0-7814-5258-9

Alpha Resources

For a complete listing and explanation of *Alpha* resources, see pages 20-21 in chapter 1 and pages 46-48 in chapter 3.

This handbook is an *Alpha* resource. The *Alpha Course* is a practical introduction to the Christian faith developed by Holy Trinity Brompton Church in London, England. *Alpha Courses* are being run worldwide.

Resources needed for setting up the *Alpha Course* (training)
• The *Alpha Course* Introductory Video (15222)
• *Alpha* Conference Tapes (16634) OR • How to Run *Alpha* Video (17178)
• *Alpha* Leaders Training Tapes(15248) OR • Training Video (25601)
• The *Alpha Course* Leader's Guide (15388: one for each Small-Group Leader and Helper)
• How to Run the *Alpha Course:* A Handbook for *Alpha* Directors, Leaders, and Helpers

Resources needed for running the *Alpha Course*
• The *Alpha Course* Tapes (16360) OR • The *Alpha Course* Videos (15149)
• The *Alpha Course* Manual (15305: one for each guest, Small-Group Leader, and Helper)
• The *Alpha Course* Leader's Guide (15388: one for each Small-Group Leader and Helper)
• Registration Brochures (15446: pack of 50)
• *Why Jesus?* (20073) OR • *Why Christmas?* (20081)
• *Questions of Life* (15396)
• *Searching Issues* (15412)

Alpha Books

by Nicky Gumbel

• ***Why Jesus?*** (20073) A booklet recommended for all participants at the start of the *Alpha Course.*

• ***Why Christmas?*** (20081) The Christmas version of *Why Jesus?*

• ***Questions of Life*** The *Alpha Course* in book form. In fifteen compelling chapters the author points the way to an authentic Christianity which is exciting and relevant to today's world.

• ***Searching Issues*** The seven issues most often raised by participants of the *Alpha Course:* suffering, other religions, sex before marriage, the New Age, homosexuality, science and Christianity, and the Trinity.

• *A Life Worth Living* What happens after *Alpha*? Based on the Book of Philippians, this is an invaluable next step for those who have just completed the *Alpha Course,* and for anyone eager to put their faith on a firm biblical footing.

• *Challenging Lifestyle* An in-depth look at the Sermon on the Mount (Matthew 5–7). The author shows that Jesus' teaching flies in the face of modern lifestyle and presents us with a radical alternative.

• *How to Run the Alpha Course: A Handbook for Alpha Directors, Leaders, and Helpers* This book includes the principles and practicalities of setting up and running an *Alpha Course.* It also includes many reproducible resources for use with *Alpha.*

In North America, all resources are published by Cook Ministry Resources, a division of Cook Communication Ministries.

To order any of the resources or books above, contact your local bookstore OR

In the USA, call or write: In Canada, call or write:

   Cook Ministry Resources   Beacon Distributing
   4050 Lee Vance View   P.O. Box 98
   Colorado Springs, CO 80918-7100   Paris, Ontario, N3L 3E5
   1-800-36-ALPHA (1-800-362-5762)   1-800-263-2664

CORRELATION OF ALPHA RESOURCES

How to Run the Alpha Course (Handbook) Title #	How to Run the Alpha Course (1 video) Session #	Alpha Conference Tapes (12 tapes) Tape #	Alpha Leaders Training Tapes (3 tapes) Tape #	Alpha Leaders Training Video (1 Video) Session #	The Alpha Course Leader's Guide Part I
1 History	—	—	—	—	—
2 Principles	1 Principles	1 Principles	—	—	—
3 Practicalities	2 Practicalities	2 Practicalities	—	—	—
4 Giving Talks					
5 Leading Small Groups		3 Small Groups and Pastoral Care	1 Leading Small Groups	1 Leading Small Groups	Part I, Session 1, p. 4
6 Pastoral Care	—	3 Small Groups and Pastoral Care	2 Pastoral Care	2 Pastoral Care	Part I, Session 2, p. 9
		4 Model Alpha Evening			
7 Ministry	—	5 Ministry during Alpha	3 Ministry	3 Ministry	Part I, Session 3, p. 13
		6 Integrating Alpha into the Church			
		7 Worship during Alpha			
		8 Daytime Alpha			
		9 Prayer during Alpha			
		10 Developing an Existing Alpha Course			
		11 Alpha Administration			
		12 Youth Alpha			

The Alpha Course

Time of Use	Talk Title	Questions of Life	Alpha Course Video/Audio Tape	Alpha Course Manual	Alpha Course Leader's Guide Part II
Alpha Dinner	Christianity: Boring, Untrue, and Irrelevant?	Chapter 1 p. 11	Talk 1	Chapter 1 p. 5	—
Week 1	Who Is Jesus?	Chapter 2 p. 23	Talk 2	Chapter 2 p. 7	Chapter 1 p. 21
Week 2	Why Did Jesus Die?	Chapter 3 p. 43	Talk 3	Chapter 3 p. 13	Chapter 2 p. 23
Week 3	How Can I Be Sure of My Faith?	Chapter 4 p. 57	Talk 4	Chapter 4 p. 16	Chapter 3 p. 26
Week 4	Why and How Should I Read the Bible?	Chapter 5 p. 69	Talk 5	Chapter 5 p. 20	Chapter 4 p. 28
Week 5	Why and How Do I Pray?	Chapter 6 p. 87	Talk 6	Chapter 6 p. 24	Chapter 5 p. 31
Week 6	How Does God Guide Us?	Chapter 7 p. 103	Talk 7	Chapter 7 p. 29	Chapter 6 p. 33
Weekend Talk 1	Who Is the Holy Spirit?	Chapter 8 p. 119	Talk 8	Chapter 8 p. 35	Chapter 7 p. 35
Weekend Talk 2	What Does the Holy Spirit Do?	Chapter 9 p. 133	Talk 9	Chapter 9 p. 40	Chapter 8 p. 36
Weekend Talk 3	How Can I Be Filled with the Spirit?	Chapter 10 p. 149	Talk 10	Chapter 10 p. 44	Chapter 9 p. 37
Weekend Talk 4	How Can I Make the Most of the Rest of My Life?	Chapter 15 p. 233	Talk 15	Chapter 15 p. 69	—
Week 7	How Can I Resist Evil?	Chapter 11 p. 165	Talk 11	Chapter 11 p. 49	Chapter 10 p. 38
Week 8	Why and How Should We Tell Others?	Chapter 12 p. 181	Talk 12	Chapter 12 p. 55	Chapter 11 p. 41
Week 9	Does God Heal Today?	Chapter 13 p. 199	Talk 13	Chapter 13 p. 59	Chapter 12 p. 43
Week 10	What About the Church?	Chapter 14 p. 217	Talk 14	Chapter 14 p. 63	Chapter 13 p. 44
Alpha Dinner	Christianity: Boring, Untrue, and Irrelevant?	Chapter 1 p. 11	Talk 1	Chapter 1 p. 5	—

APPENDIX G: SUGGESTED READING & ALPHA RESOURCES

Alpha Copyright Statement

1. All *Alpha* resources and materials, including manuals, tapes, videos, and graphics are strictly copyrighted to Holy Trinity Brompton Church in London, England, with the exception of books published by either Kingsway or Cook Communications Ministries in which the author is stated to hold the copyright.

2. No part of any *Alpha* resource may be reproduced or transmitted in any form or by any means, electronic or mechanical, including photocopying, recording, translating, or any information storage and retrieval system without permission in writing from the publisher: Cook Communications Ministries; 4050 Lee Vance View; Colorado Springs, CO, 80918-7100, USA.

3. Use of the *Alpha* logo is permitted only in conjunction with the running or promotion of an *Alpha Course*. Resale or the obtaining of payment in return for use of the logo or obtaining of monies in any other connection with the logo is forbidden.

4. Holy Trinity Brompton asks that the names *"Alpha," "Alpha Course,"* or similar names, not be used in conjunction with any other Christian course or the promotion thereof. This is in order to avoid a situation where many different courses have similar titles, thereby causing confusion and uncertainty as to what the *Alpha Course* really is. This request is made simply to ensure that participants are receiving only *Alpha* teaching.

5. As an exception to paragraph 2 above, Holy Trinity Brompton will allow minor adaptations to be made to the *Alpha Course* in the situation and in the manner detailed below:

The *Alpha Course* may be altered as stated below, provided that the person developing the altered version neither uses nor promotes such a course outside his or her home church or parish. No other person may so use or promote such an altered course. The altered course must be confined to the church or parish of the person who developed it.

The *Alpha Course* may be shortened or lengthened by varying the length of the talks. Not all the material must be used, additional material may be used. This is subject to the proviso that such alterations do not change the essential character of the course. *Alpha* is designed to be a series of fifteen talks, over a period of time, including a weekend or a day spent together, and teaching on all the topics contained in *Questions of Life* (Nicky Gumbel, David C. Cook Publishing Company). This teaching should neither be departed from nor qualitatively altered in an *Alpha Course* for the reason in paragraph 4 above. The material should not be reproduced in part or in whole without the permission in writing from the publisher per paragraph 2 above.

This statement supersedes all previous statements relating to copyright in any *Alpha Course*. August 1997.